Praise for *Breathing Life Into Your Characters*

Breathing Life Into Your Characters is a comprehensive and incisive look at creating characters whose words, deeds, actions/reactions, and feelings will leap off the page, leaving an indelible, believable, and memorable impression! Kudos to Rachel "Doc Hollywood" Ballon! —Kathie Fong Yoneda, Paramount Pictures story analyst/development specialist and author of *The Script Selling Game*

Better than anyone I know, Rachel Ballon understands the confluence of good character writing and psychology. It's a good thing for the mental health of writers and audiences that she's set down her insights about how awareness of the inner, personal drama really does breathe life into fictional characters.

Writers simply can't write beyond the limits of their own psychological growth, but this book shows them how to break through by tapping the power of their emotions. It gives them the courage to dig deeper in their writing and make it more honest and psychologically solid.—Chris Vogler, screenwriter and author of *The Writer's Journey: Mythic Structure for Writers*

Creating compelling characters is the key to writing a novel that readers care about or a screenplay that attracts the stars who get movies made. In this profoundly insightful exploration of the psychology of fictional characters, Rachel Ballon clearly explains how to do just that. But she goes one important step further by showing writers how to explore their own psychology and apply that to the characters who are so much a part of themselves.
—Pamela Wallace, Academy Award-winning screenwriter for *Witness* and author of more than twenty-four novels

Breathing Life Into Your Characters is a writer's gold mine. Writers who read this book, study it, and do the exercises will tap deeply into their ability to create emotionally deeper, more realistic, compelling characters. Dr. Ballon has written a remarkable and necessary book that will nurture all writers.—Dr. Linda Seger, author of *Creating Unforgettable Characters* and *Advanced Screenwriting*

Breathing Life Into Your Characters

Breathing *life* into your *characters*

Rachel Ballon, Ph.D.

WRITER'S DIGEST BOOKS
CINCINNATI, OH
WWW.WRITERSDIGEST.COM

Breathing Life Into Your Characters. Copyright © 2003 by Rachel Ballon, Ph.D. Manufactured in the United States of America. All rights reserved. No part of this book may be reproduced in any form or by any electronic or mechanical means including information storage and retrieval systems without permission in writing from the publisher, except by a reviewer, who may quote brief passages in a review. Published by Writer's Digest Books, an imprint of F&W Publications, Inc., 4700 East Galbraith Road, Cincinnati, Ohio 45236. (800) 289-0963. First edition.

Visit our Web site at www.writersdigest.com for information on more resources for writers.

To receive a free weekly e-mail newsletter delivering tips and updates about writing and about Writer's Digest products, register directly at our Web site at http://newsletters.fwpublications.com.

07 06 05 04 03   5 4 3 2 1

Library of Congress Cataloging-in-Publication Data

Ballon, Rachel Friedman
   Breathing life into your characters : how to give your characters emotional and psychological depth / by Rachel Ballon.
      p.   cm.
   Includes index.
   ISBN 1-58297-181-1 (alk. paper)
      1. Fiction—Technique. 2. Characters and characteristics in literature. I. Title.

PN3383.C4B35   2003
808.3—dc21   2003057560
                                                               CIP

Edited by Kelly Nickell
Designed by Sandy Kent
Cover by Andrea Short
Production coordinated by Sara Dumford

To my children
Marc, Amy, John
With love

About the Author

Dr. Rachel Ballon is a recognized psychotherapist who specializes in working with writers. She is also an international writing consultant. She brings her expertise in both fields to her seminars and private practice. As the founder/director of The Writer's Center in Los Angeles, she consults with writers on a one-on-one basis and conducts classes on journal writing. A former adjunct professor at the highly respected University of Southern California School of Cinema and Television, she has conducted writing workshops throughout the United States and Europe. She is the author of the widely acclaimed *Blueprint for Writing* and *The Writer's Sourcebook*. She lives in Los Angeles, California.

For additional information about the author, visit her Web site at www.rachelballon.com or e-mail her at rachwrite@aol.com.

To learn more about individual consultations with Dr. Ballon or for more information about The Writer's Center, call (310) 472-8442.

Acknowledgments

Writing a book is giving birth to an entity that never existed. It is first conceived with an idea and then nurtured along the way with support, encouragement, and love. Special recognition must be given to those people who provided their support, encouragement, and love. The passion for this book was first borne when I taught a one-day workshop called "Beneath the Mask: Creating Characters From the Inside Out" and saw firsthand how valuable it can be for writers to go inside themselves to mine the gems of their creativity. Thank you to Linda Venis, head of the highly-esteemed extension UCLA Writer's Program who gave me this opportunity to share my vision with thousands of writers throughout the years.

A chance conversation with Jack Heffron at Writer's Digest Books gave me this opportunity to take my vision and make it a reality. He and I are of like minds, and his enthusiasm for the subject of creating characters from the inside was contagious and validated my vision. I will be forever grateful to him for his huge contribution to starting the process.

My appreciation and thanks go to my editor, Kelly Nickell. Her notes, suggestions, and knowledge vastly contributed to the final results of the book. Thanks to Meg Leder, who did a comprehensive job as copy editor.

Without the love of both family and friends, giving birth to a book would be a lonely process. Luckily, I wasn't alone. A loving thank-you to my husband, Bill. I am forever grateful for his constant belief in the importance of the material and for his willingness to listen to new ideas. A big thank-you to my children—Marc, Amy, and John for their support and love, and also the invaluable writing suggestions from my writer sons, Marc and John. Love and hugs to wonderful Brittany and Bradley for being just the way you are. And thanks to Robin for her interest.

A grateful thank-you to my sister and brother, Linda and Howard Mann, for their generosity and love, and especially for the R & R in Hawaii. Thanks to my nephew Josh Mann, a talented actor, who shared some of his favorite books with me as resources. And to my nephew Matt Mann, for being you.

A heartfelt thank-you also goes to Martine Ehrenclou, a beautiful writer and friend who was always available with encouragement and support. I am grateful for the time you spent helping me find a few of the perfect excerpts for this book.

To Brenda Krantz, a dear friend, collaborator, and wonderful playwright, I thank you for your belief and enthusiasm from the very first time I told you about the book—it was energizing.

I am most appreciative to Joan Dasteel for always being there with her support. Thank you for teaching me how to receive your kindness.

A big thank-you goes to Donie Nelson, a consultant for writers and a friend, who over lunch one day suggested the book's great title—*Breathing Life Into Your Characters*.

Thanks to Judith Merians, for her continuous interest regarding the progress of the book and her sage advice. To my friends Adrienne Fayne and Sue Blum—thanks for being there.

Thank you to my fellow writing consultants and colleagues for their support and friendship: to Kathy Fong Yoneda for her heart, to Linda Seger for her faith, and to Carolyn Miller for her wisdom.

To my beloved friend Betty Barry who introduced me to the Friends of the Beverly Hills Library. It was from their wonderful bookstore that I found so many treasured gems for the book. I miss you.

And to all of my writing students and therapy clients who shared their most precious possession with me—themselves. You taught me that all creative individuals need to reach inside to discover their inner beauty. Thank you for your stories from your heart.

Table of Contents

Introduction

I have tried every device I know to breathe life into my characters, for there is little in fiction more rewarding than to see real people interact on a page. —*James A. Michener*

*W*hen I was in graduate school studying to become a psychotherapist, I used to make a weekly visit to the local bookstore. I was always torn between whether to buy a writing book or a psychology book. After pouring through the recently published books in each subject, I usually ended up purchasing several books in both fields, since I equally loved writing and psychology.

Many years later, the bookcases in my office are filled with books on each subject, and my love of literature and psychology has turned out to be a marriage made in heaven. As a psychotherapist who specializes in writers and as a writing consultant who has helped thousands of writers build fascinating characters through the use of psychology, I continue to combine my two interests to get the best results for my writing clients.

The two fields are very compatible, intricately bound, and synergistic. During the years I've taught writers how to create characters from the inside out, I've stressed emotional conflicts, the human condition, personal relationships, personality, inner motivation, self-esteem—all elements that deal with psychology. When I listen to clients in my private therapy practice relate their personal stories, they have a narrative structure just as a fictional story does: a main character with a goal who encounters obstacles in her life script.

Writing is much more powerful than talking because it provides readers with direct access to an individual's inner world. I use the therapeutic writing exercises I've developed in my counseling practice even with nonwriters, and the results are astounding in creating positive change and personal growth.

As the author of two nonfiction books (*Blueprint for Writing* and *The Writer's Sourcebook*), a published poet, a novelist, and a scriptwriter, I've been fortunate to find a career path where writing and psychology have been so intimately interwoven into my life. It is with this passion for psychology and enthusiasm for writing that I've written *Breathing Life Into Your Characters*.

My approach for working with writers has always been to help them focus on developing in-depth and emotional characters by teaching them to understand psychology—their own and that of their characters—through various techniques that guide them in how to reach deep inside themselves, and, in turn, deep inside their characters.

Modern day audiences are psychologically savvy and sophisticated, forcing writers to delve into the psychology of their characters like never before. Just look at talk shows such as *The Oprah Winfrey Show*, *The Montel Williams Show*, and *Jenny Jones*, where a proliferation of psychologists inform studio and television audiences about all types of psychological problems and traumas. These psychologists discuss topics as diverse as living alone, children who kill children, single parenting, love and marriage, sexual abuse, physical abuse, emotional abuse, drug addiction, alcoholism, problem relationships, and dysfunctional families.

To be an effective writer of any form or genre, you must create believable, credible, and realistic characters to make your story work. And you can only truly breathe life into your characters by having a real knowledge of human nature, mental health issues, and basic psychology.

I have spent the past twenty years working as a licensed psychotherapist and as a writing consultant teaching the principles of craft and structure in workshops. Based on this experience, it is my belief that dealing only with the elements of dialogue, theme, structure, plot, story, characters, setting, and conflict is not enough. Many writers master craft, but still write stories and scripts without heart. Although their structure is solid and their dialogue is strong, their characters are weak, flat, and stereotypical. Powerful writing has to originate from the inside out, and yet many talented writers have no idea how to use their own psychology and feelings to create characters with emotional depth. Craft without heart simply isn't enough.

In an effort to show writers how to reconnect with their most potent resource—their inner self—I developed a writing workshop called "Beneath the Mask: Creating Characters From the Inside Out," which I taught at the UCLA Writer's Program in extension and at the USC School of Cinema and Television. In both workshops, my goal was for students to learn to use their own psychology through self-exploration of their inner world and to weave their emotions into their fictional characters.

It was amazing how quickly the individual students began to use their own material to build characters who were original and emotionally powerful.

One particular student, whom I'll call Betty, was a prolific writer with great ideas for stories and plots. Unfortunately, even though she had studied craft and understood story structure, her scripts were always flat, and her characters were bland. She desperately wanted to give her characters more feelings, but she just wasn't able to do it. By the time I met her she had taken every writing workshop available in Los Angeles.

However, once she began to examine her own psychology and eventually learned how to tap into her own emotions, her writing dramatically improved, and her characters became more emotional. Why? Because she had the courage to create characters from the inside out. Within a few months she began to sell her writing and has had continued success ever since.

The results of these workshops were astounding for everyone! Writers who were willing to look inside to understand their own psychological makeup began to give birth to characters with inner conflicts just like their own. Their characters became complex rather than one-dimensional, layered rather than superficial, bold rather than bland.

Breathing Life Into Your Characters will provide you with the necessary tools and techniques you'll need to create outstanding characters who evolve from the inside out. Become introspective, and you'll be able to unleash torrents of feelings and get them on the page through your characters. By reading this book, you'll be able to look behind your character's facade to find the real person inside and what makes him tick.

A psychologist's job is to make sense of aberrant behavior by asking the big question: Why? Why does an intelligent woman stay with a man who beats her? Why do individuals destroy their lives and the lives of others? Why does a beloved teacher become a child molester? Why does a politician risk his career through nefarious or illicit behavior? Why does a quiet kid kill his classmates and his parents? Why can't people control their hidden urges, their distorted thinking, or their inner drives, which lead to deviant or self-destructive behavior? Why do human beings ruin their lives, their reputations, and their families?

In *Breathing Life Into Your Characters*, these are the exact same questions you will ask and answer for all of your fictional characters. To become a realistic and dramatic writer, you'll need to think like a psychologist and ask probing questions of your characters in order to have a better understanding of their inner lives. You'll have to discover what urges and thoughts drive your characters to behave as they do. Through a developed knowledge of psychology, you'll learn how to internally motivate your characters' external goals.

In this book, you will learn how to use visualization, guided imagery, and writing exercises to tap your unconscious and use those insights for creating characters. You'll also discover how to internally motivate your characters and to make their behavior believable by answering the "why" for all of their actions.

In addition, you'll discover how to develop psychological makeups of your characters, as well as how to explore their internal conflicts and interpersonal relationships. In order to create original, complicated, and unique characters, you'll need to recognize the role conflict plays in motivating and driving the internal desires and goals of individual characters. You'll also learn how to give your characters realistic defense mechanisms so that they can cope with conflict in an honest and believable manner.

The exercises in this book will teach you how to explore your emotional memories so you'll be able to inject your feelings into your characters and onto the page. You'll discover how to use your feelings to give characters heart and soul. Through developing characters' nonverbal communication and body language, you'll also allow them to silently express their emotions and attitudes toward one another, showing rather than telling the reader what your characters are thinking.

By reading *Breathing Life Into Your Characters* and completing the writing exercises, you'll understand how to use psychological principles to build believable and complex characters who are well-rounded human beings with a dramatic "ring of truth."

writing characters from the inside out

Human beings, by changing the inner attitudes of their minds,
can change the outer aspects of their lives. —*William James*

*M*any writers have a difficult time creating believable and
unique characters, rather than stock and stereotypical characters. Some people do extensive research outside themselves, trying to
find the right elements for developing exciting and multifaceted characters. But research alone won't solve the problem because the essential
components for creating successful characters with emotional and psychological depth—feelings, passion, desires, psychology, and vision—
reside within.

All meaningful writing must connect to your inner world. Anyone
can learn craft, but it takes more than structure to make your writing
and your characters work. I have read scripts and manuscripts, short
stories, and plays in which the characters displayed no hint of spirit,
originality, or truth. The secret to having your characters stand out
from all the rest is to put your heart and spirit into them. You can't
write effectively until you are able to experience your inner self in the
process of creating characters. You need to be present in your characters and in your writing or your story will fail. Your audience must
be able to hear your voice as that of the narrator and not as a detached
or distant chronicler or historian. And you need to create different
characters to express your various voices.

The only difference between a mediocre character who has been portrayed hundreds of times and a unique, fresh, original character is you. It's imperative to let yourself be vulnerable, receptive and open to taking risks in your writing. You must explore your inner self in order to reach into your life experiences, especially those of your childhood, and to try to recapture your original feelings. By learning how to create characters from your inner self, you'll unlock your sensory memories and transform them into unique and original characters capable of touching the hearts of your audience.

However, this is often easier said than done. As small children we learn to develop a facade or mask to protect us from hurt or from getting into trouble. We learn how to behave by the rules and to harness emotions that might have caused us problems in the past. As adults, most of us have lost our connection to our core or real self, and many of us have become alienated from our inner world.

It's true that many of us begin to suppress our true nature and conform to what best serves us, until we unfortunately lose who we really are. But this can change when you write. By breathing life into your characters, you'll reconnect to your wellspring of memories, emotions, and childhood experiences to discover the many new voices within. If you don't journey beneath your mask to find the real you, you can't explore your original voices. Allow these voices to speak from the inside and let them sing through your fictional characters.

Since powerful characterization needs to come from within, no number of courses, books, or seminars on character development will improve your work until you are able to fully explore your inner self and release your characters. When you write only from your ego or your conscious mind, you are just touching the tip of the iceberg. However, if you plumb the depths inside, you will find unique characters and interesting stories. A courageous writer writes from his inner self. Remember, you can't give to your characters what you can't give to yourself. If you have disowned and removed yourself from your past and your powerful memories, how will you be able to have your characters experience feelings you refuse to acknowledge? Let's discuss the unconscious and how important a part it plays in creating complex characters.

The Unconscious

When I feel difficulty coming on, I switch to another book I'm writing. When I get back to the problem, my unconscious has solved it. —*Isaac Asimov*

To be a writer is to embrace being in your unconscious and to get joy from being there. Writing is a lifestyle of its own—tapping one's inner world. Most writers don't write from their inner characters and stories. Instead, they write from the outside in, looking for external characters and plots, and their writing, as a result, is shallow and clichéd. A writer must look deeper into the inner world of characters to penetrate the recesses of human nature. Somewhere in your psyche is a wealth of information about everything that's ever happened to you—it's yours for the taking, if you can overcome your resistance and start tapping into your rich and alive unconscious.

According to Sigmund Freud, the father of psychoanalysis, the unconscious is a repository for our repressed memories and emotions, especially ones that are too traumatic to remember. We are not aware of our buried memories and feelings, even though they often influence our present behavior without our awareness. For example, suppose you are always late despite your most sincere efforts to be on time. This self-defeating behavior could be due to something in your childhood where you had to operate on a rigid time schedule. Perhaps you're unconsciously rebelling. As far as you're consciously concerned, you truly don't want to be late, but something always interferes and prevents you from being on time.

The same can be true when it comes to writing. You desperately want to create exciting characters and stories, but you're always procrastinating and feeling miserable because you're not writing. You promise that you'll write tomorrow, but tomorrow comes and you still aren't writing. Perhaps you have a fear of failure or rejection, so what better way to avoid both than by not writing. This is your unconscious way of protecting yourself—after all, if you don't write, you don't get hurt. Unless you start consciously working to retrieve your repressed feelings, they'll remain forever buried in the deep recesses of your mind, and your cast of characters will remain silent.

Free Your Repressed Memories

To withdraw myself from myself has ever been my sole, my entire, my sincere motive in scribbling at all.—*Lord Byron*

Recently, I met with a children's writer who was working on a young adult novel. She was having trouble portraying the main character whose mother had died. The writer wasn't able to translate her teenage character's grief for his mother into believable behavior or dialogue.

The main character, the son, had no reaction to his mother's death and just hung out with his friends as if nothing happened. I told her that unless she could give her main character a realistic reaction to his mother's death, the entire story wouldn't work from that point on. Together we worked on the character to develop believable reactions to the mother's death. Try as she may, however, the writer still wasn't able to give her teenage boy any realistic emotions.

I referred her to a book called *On Death and Dying* by psychiatrist Elisabeth Kübler-Ross, who brought attention to personalizing death rather than denying it. Briefly stated, her theory focuses on the five stages of the grieving process—denial, anger, bargaining, depression, and acceptance (we'll discuss these further in chapter nine). My hope was that by giving my client some psychological material to work with, she'd be able to create a character who experienced the grieving

FREEWRITING

Write as freely and as rapidly as possible and throw the whole thing on paper. Never correct or rewrite until the whole thing is down.
—John Steinbeck

When you first begin to write, concentrate on the writing process itself and not on the technique. Write your ideas without worrying whether they're good enough. By staying in the moment, your writing will flow. This method of writing from your inner world is the first burst of imagination that comes to you in a moment of inspiration. It's known as free or automatic writing because you write without worrying about grammar, spelling, or punctuation. Just keep the pen moving and don't lift it from the page for at least fifteen minutes.

The amazing phenomenon about freewriting is that the words flow from the pen naturally and unrestricted by thought, making them rich in emotion and description. Since freewriting taps into your uninhibited inner truths, your writing will have a more definite shape and be filled with specificity, and your characters will have a depth and honesty as never before.

Since many of the writing exercises presented in this book draw on freewriting techniques, the exercises enable you to reach your inner depths and mine the buried treasure within. They allow you to awaken your inner characters and transform them into fascinating fictional characters. By working through the writing exercises, you'll go on a journey to relive and emotionally reexperience your childhood stories, memories, and feelings through the use of visualization and writing. ·∾·

process. But this approach didn't work either, and her main character's behavior remained stilted.

During the author's next appointment, I had her recall a time she'd experienced a loss in her life. She related the death of her beloved grandfather, and as she told me about his funeral she was completely detached of emotions. It was then that I realized that in order for her to give her character emotion, she needed to open herself up to her own feelings of grief and loss.

The lesson here is this: The only way you'll have any success in creating realistic characters is if you reconnect to your own feelings first. Unfortunately, many of us don't want to work through our repressed memories, so we unconsciously put up barriers that stop us from looking inside ourselves. We have to deal with this dichotomy each time we start to write because there is always that fine line between writing what you know and feel passionate about and being so close to your material so that you can't be objective and let the feelings flow.

Creating fictional characters with feelings similar to your own often gives you the opportunity to work through a problem on a trial basis. You can use your characters in conflict as a "dress rehearsal" for future actions you'll take in your own life. I have seen many writers get more therapeutic benefits through writing than through therapy! Let's see if you can reconnect with some of your own emotions in the following exercise.

EXERCISE
Tapping Into Your Memories

Recall a time when you experienced an emotionally powerful event in your life. It could be the loss of somebody you loved or a painful breakup. Before you begin to write, try to relax by concentrating on breathing deeply. You may also want to play some peaceful or meditative music. After you're completely relaxed, begin to write. Write about the experience in the present tense, using first person and your senses of touch, taste, sound, sight, and smell. Describe your sensory memory of the smell of the room, the texture of the wood, the color of the flowers, your feelings about the experience, the expression on your face, etc.

Freewrite as fast as you can without worrying about grammar, spelling, or punctuation. Above all, keep the pen moving. Don't lift the pen from the page until you've written for at least fifteen minutes. The words should come tumbling from your pen.

Once you've finished, consider the following: During the writing process were you able to enter your emotional memory of a highly charged life experience from your past? Did you reexperience your feelings? Were you surprised at what situation came up for you? Had you forgotten about it or not thought about it for years? What emotions did you experience while writing? Now that you've accessed your feelings put them into your fictional characters when you want to create characters with similar emotions.

The client I mentioned just before the start of this exercise chose to write about the day of her grandfather's funeral and how scared she'd been when she saw his body in the open casket. As she read what she'd written, the tears started to pour down her cheeks and she suddenly burst into such heart-wrenching sobs, it was impossible for her to continue.

The exercise allowed her to emotionally relive the memory of her grandfather's death. As she wrote, her dormant feelings were released through her five senses. After reexperiencing her own painful emotions about death, she freed her pent-up sorrow and freely wrote it into her fictional teenage character. He became realistic because she gave him reactions that were honest and allowed her readers to feel empathy for him. ■ ■ ■

Collective Unconscious

> In all chaos there is a cosmos, in all disorder a secret order.
> —*C.G. Jung*

On the other hand, Swiss psychiatrist C.G. Jung, a disciple of Freud, disagreed. Although Jung believed in the unconscious, his theory also included what he called the "collective unconscious." According to Jung, the collective unconscious contains primordial images that have been passed down by our ancestors from generation to generation. Inside the collective unconscious reside archetypes, or universal characters, that have been imprinted. They represent aspects of our personality and the human condition that relate to our species.

Archetypes give our characters and stories deeper meaning and stimulate our imaginations. Myths and fairy tales are filled with archetypal characters such as the the wicked witch, the handsome hero or prince, or the good fairy and dwarfs. I will discuss archetypes in greater detail in chapter four.

The essential decision to be an emotional writer means making a commitment to yourself and saying, "I'm going to be a person of my unconscious. I'm going to listen to it and express it and live in it." Once you are aware of your unconscious and you're willing to explore it through self-discovery, your characters will develop more depth. You're using the most potent creative resource available to create rich, emotional characters—yourself.

The "Aha" Moment

Nothing great was ever achieved without enthusiasm.
—*Ralph Waldo Emerson*

When you first start to write, you need to write from your intuition and get your thoughts down before you apply left-brain logic and organization to your work. Creating characters from your emotional side allows you to forget judgments and listen to your instincts. Trust your "gut" feelings about your characters, and you'll develop complex and colorful ones for your stories.

If you write from the unconscious, time disappears and you become unaware of your past or future. You just experience the moment. That's when poetry, music, spirit, imagination, and creativity emerge, along with exciting ideas for characters and stories. This moment of inspiration is what is referred to as that wonderful "Aha" moment, when you're transported to a higher level of creativity. You may look at the clock after "a few minutes" of writing only to find hours have gone by. In such instances you were writing in the moment, totally immersed and absorbed in the present. You were involved in the process of writing rather than in the results.

All dramatic emotional characters are created on this level of the unconscious, which allows you to write from your visual brain to recall past events and remember childhood stories in sensory detail. Writing from your unconscious enables you to retrieve the emotional and personal experiences of your forgotten memories.

To be successful at creating realistic and layered characters, you must be willing and unafraid to connect with your inner characters. If you're coming from your ego when you write, you're missing the magic and music that appears from your deeper self. By being willing to reach down into your unconscious, you'll give your fictional characters greater dimension, complexities, and human qualities (warts and all).

You must be present when you create characters from the inside because you *are* all the characters. Be open to your inside material, and let yourself become vulnerable and receptive to taking risks. To be a forceful writer you must learn to reveal yourself—the good, the bad, and the ugly. Try not to conceal yourself. It's important for you to tap into your unconscious and connect with the wellsprings of your deeper truths and creativity. Give these feelings to your characters, so your writing has a purpose and meaning that connects to your audience.

EXERCISE
Visualization and Guided Imagery

Visualization is the technique of imagining visual pictures. It closes off the left hemisphere of your brain and lets the right

hemisphere express insights without criticism. Visualization allows you to write with creative energy, inspiration, and imagery. Visualization also involves the exploration of pictures that come to your mind, allowing you to experience a kind of waking dream. Combined with freewriting, visualization offers a direct path to the unconscious and to your buried treasures—emotions, feelings, memories. The following technique shows you how to use visualization before you begin to write.

First you need to get comfortable, close your eyes, and begin to breathe deeply. Continue breathing until you feel the muscles in your body completely relax. Next, visualize yourself as a small child. Picture yourself in a natural setting such as in a meadow, the woods, a park, or by the ocean.

Say that you've chosen to visualize a time in your childhood when you were at an ocean. As you visualize the setting, stay in the scene with all of your senses. Smell the sea air, listen to the birds singing, touch the hot sand, taste the salty water, and see the myriad colors of the ocean. Get into the scene and imagine yourself there in the present moment. What are you wearing? How does your hair look blowing in the breeze? What expression do you have on your face? Are you alone or with a friend? What does the ocean smell like, taste like, feel like? Take a few more moments and visualize every detail with all of your senses. What are you feeling in this wonderful natural setting? Are you happy? Sad? Lonely? Playful? Carefree? Experience every detail with your sensory memory and your emotions.

Now take your pen and notebook and start writing about the experience as fast as you can. Using first person present tense, write with all your senses and describe the visual pictures you've just experienced. Remember not to stop writing until you've written for fifteen or twenty minutes. After you've finished writing, read what you've written aloud to another person. Choose someone you trust who will just listen without criticism or judgment, someone who will hear your words and help you articulate what you are trying to express. This exercise uses the written word to help you access characters from the inside.

Writing without any type of rules or structure enables you to access the power of the unconscious and recall dramatic stories and memories from your past. Now see if you can take what you've written and turn it into a story.

You'll also be amazed at the powerful characters and picturesque scenes you'll write in such a short amount of time. And it's all possible because you've closed off the critical and judgmental part of your brain and are writing from your uncensored unconscious using a combination of visualization and free writing. ■ ■ ■

Dreams

> **In bed my real love has always been the sleep that rescued me by allowing me to dream.**—*Luigi Pirandello*

Another way to tap into your unconscious material is through your dreams. Dreams are important guides to tell you what's going on in your unconscious. Our dreams are messages from the deeper levels of our personalities. In *The Interpretation of Dreams*, Freud wrote that he believed dreams represented unconscious wish fulfillment. According to Freud, dreams express the unconscious wishes and repressed sexual desires buried deep in our psyche. As a writer, there is a lot to learn from analyzing your dreams and using aspects of them in your writing, especially when you create characters based on your dreams. By doing so, you're uncovering concealed meanings in your dreams and your characters will symbolize them.

On the other hand, Jung postulated in his theory on dreams that they did not represent repressed material. From his *Collected Works*, Jung wrote: "The dream is specifically the utterance of the unconscious mind. Just as the psyche has a diurnal side which we call consciousness, so also it has a nocturnal side, the unconscious psyche activity which we apprehend as dreamlike fantasy."

Jung further disagreed with Freud's belief that dreams were symbols that conceal real meaning, saying: "It is characteristic of dreams to present pictorial and picturesque language to colorless and merely rational statements. This is certainly not an intentional concealment; it simply emphasizes our inability to understand the emotionally charged picture language of dreams."

In addition, Jung also stressed the importance of creativity and believed if writers could access their dreams and their collective unconscious they would be able to create characters who are archetypal and with whom readers and viewers would relate. It's important for you to retrieve emotional material from your dreams to use in creating characters who are original and emotional, while, at the same time, universal.

Whether you adhere to Freud or Jung's theory on dreams, dreams are a wonderfully rich resource for creating characters and stories. Trust that your dreams come from your own imagination and creativity and you'll discover hidden treasures in them for new characters and exciting ideas for stories.

EXERCISE

Dream Journaling to Unlock Your Inner Creativity

If you seriously want to mine your inner stories and write with depth, keep a dream journal and record your dreams as soon as you awaken. Keep a notebook and pen by your bed so that you can remember the dream even if it's vague, because if you wait too long the dream will usually be forgotten. The benefits from keeping a dream journal are twofold. First, it will help you connect to your inner world, your fantasy life, and your creativity. Second, you'll be surprised to discover not only more self-knowledge, but new material for future stories from your dreams.

As you begin to record your dreams, take note of any recurring character who appears. Write in detail about the character and what he or she means to you. Are you aware of a recurring relationship in your dream (mother, father, son, brother, girlfriend, sister)? Describe the relationship and the meaning behind it. Have you discovered anything new about yourself through your dreams? If yes, write about what has changed for you—in both yourself and in your life. Remember, your dreams are a direct path to your characters, so what changes for you also changes for them. ■ ■ ■

Write What You Feel, Not What You Know

Wrestling with words gave me my moments of greatest meaning.—*Richard Wright*

When I say to "write what you know," I don't want to be taken literally. What I do want is for you to get in touch with your varied feelings and write about them, so your characters will become authentic human beings.

My motto for writers is: "Don't write what you know; write what you feel."

Creating fictional characters with feelings similar to your own often gives you the opportunity to work through a problem on a trial basis. In order to write well-rounded, three-dimensional, realistic characters, you must *first* find your own unique voice, the one buried inside behind your facade. You must voyage deep into your inner world to a place where you're truly able to reexperience childhood memories and emotions, and reach the parts of yourself that have been sleeping for years.

The act of writing in a journal—a journal separate from the dream journal mentioned earlier—helps you make this connection to your inner self. Recollections of memories and self-exploration of your life stories can enable you to right the wrongs of your past and practice future behaviors. Exploring your life through journaling also can help you to live your life from the inside out and not from the outside in. When you get in the habit of writing in your journal every day, you'll become aware of possible characters and plots for your fictional stories as you become more and more familiar with the people and plot lines existing in your true reality.

As you begin your journey of self-discovery and reconnect to feelings, emotions, and attitudes buried in your unconscious, magic begins to happen with your characters. As you reacquaint yourself with the dormant powerful selves living inside, you'll experience a sense of renewal and rebirth. Taking back these parts of yourself gives you a feeling of homecoming and reunion. And by taking the most exciting journey of your life—the journey into yourself—you'll discover a reservoir of characters at your disposal.

ghosts of the past: your characters' backstories

If the writing is honest it cannot be separated from the man who wrote it. —*Tennessee Williams*

*M*ost stories start somewhere in the middle of the characters' lives, when a dramatic question, inciting incident, or crisis sets up the story. Everything that has happened to the characters before the story opens is known as the backstory. This includes all the events, life experiences, memories, and childhood incidents that make up the characters' past.

After you decide when you're going to open your story, choose the characters you need to carry out the story, and determine your main character, you'll want to create their backgrounds. Just as in your own life when you bring the ghosts of the past to your personal and professional relationships, your characters also bring ghosts of the past to their relationships. In order for you to properly develop their backstories, you'll need to free these ghosts.

Past information gets revealed as relationships become more personal and intimacy levels increase. In essence, as you make friends or enemies, people learn more about your backstory, just as they learn about your character's backstory through his relationships. Whether you write children's books, short stories, plays, scripts, or novels, when you begin your story you need to create characters who will carry out the plot.

Before you do this, however, you first need to determine who your main character is. Your main character should have a specific goal, desire, or intention that he has to reach by the end of the story. By undertaking this central journey, your main character also should experience an emotional transformation by the story's end.

Never create a character who doesn't relate to or is not involved with your main character's goal. All your characters should serve the main story line and move your story forward. These characters will provide conflicts and emotional relationships, create obstacles, or become allies.

That said, it's important for you to develop a character biography for your main and major characters in order to give them rich backstories. But don't stop there. In addition to creating individual character biographies, you must also dig deeper inside yourself so all your characters have depth and dimension.

Exploring Your Past

The past is never dead. It's not even the past.
—*William Faulkner*

As the creator of all your characters, you need to explore your own self before you explore your characters. Whether your characters are twenty-five or seventy-five years old, it's essential for you to know about their childhood, family, and emotional experiences long before your story opens. This is true even if the audience never learns the information during the story. Even though some information will go unstated, it will still help you to create more vivid and fully realized characters.

Before you begin to build a backstory, you must open yourself up for your characters by answering questions not only about your characters, but also about yourself. After all, how can you give to your characters what you can't give to yourself?

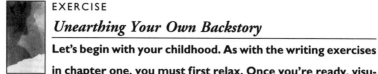

EXERCISE

Unearthing Your Own Backstory

Let's begin with your childhood. As with the writing exercises in chapter one, you must first relax. Once you're ready, visualize and revisit your childhood using your five senses. Write in first person and present tense. Recall a specific time that illustrates how your family interacted with one another. Maybe it's a holiday, or maybe it's dinnertime. Do you remember how old you were? Write for at least fifteen minutes. When you're finished read aloud what you've written.

How do your words make you feel? Does this childhood memory give you an idea for developing a story or script? For creating original characters? When you start to remember your past, you will discover a wealth of material just waiting to be transformed into stories. Think about all the stories and films that are set around a dinner or holiday, and how much such scenes can reveal about the people involved.

Now, try writing about how you felt coming in the door after school. How did you expect to be greeted? Did you feel happy, fearful, sad? What did you talk about to your friends when you were little? What kind of games did you play? Were you popular or picked on in school? Did you have a lot of friends or were you a loner? Were you the last person chosen to be on the baseball team or the first? Write your memories and see what they reveal about who you were and who you've become. Once you begin writing, remember to keep the pen moving for at least fifteen to twenty minutes.

As you answer these questions, keep digging deeper into your childhood memories. There is nobody on earth like you, so why not put your memories, experiences, and personal passions into your characters? Use this raw material as a jumping-off point for your characters. ■ ■ ■

Exploring Your Character's Past

If you can tell stories, create characters, devise incidents, and have sincerity and passion, it doesn't matter a damn how you write.—*W. Somerset Maugham*

Now that you've explored your past, create character biographies to explore the pasts of your characters. Developing a character biography is the first step in helping you have a better understanding of who your characters are. A character biography is exactly what it says—a personal history and inventory of your character's traits, physical makeup, and personality. To get better acquainted with your characters, understand what motivates their behavior. To accomplish this, you need to develop your character biographies using three categories: the physical, the social, and the emotional. As you investigate each category, you'll become more familiar with each of your characters.

The Physical

The physical aspects of your characters are rather basic. They include their height, weight, hair, and eye color. You'll develop how each character walks, talks, eats, and smiles, along with any distinct mannerisms, gestures, and posturing. What is your character's overall appearance? Is he handsome, ugly, weak, strong, stocky, fat, thin?

When creating your character's physical traits, try to anticipate what important traits he'll need for his role in the plot. Take, for example, Dorothy Allison's novel *Bastard Out of Carolina*. In the book, the narrator, a young girl named Ruth Anne Boatwright, known as Bone, describes the man who will soon become her stepfather, Glen Waddell. His physical appearance is important to the role he'll later play in being abusive to her:

> Glen was a small man but so muscular and strong that it was
> hard to see the delicacy in him, though he was strangely graceful

in his rough work clothes and heavy boots. . . . Glen Waddell's feet were so fine that his boots had to be bought in the boys' department of Sears, Roebuck, while his gloves could only be found in the tall men's specialty stores. He would pivot on those boy-size-feet, turning his narrow hips and grunting with his load, everything straining and forceful, while his hands cradled cases and flats as delicately as if they were soft-shelled eggs.

Your characters' choices and decisions determine the plot. Even if you have a particular story in mind first, you still need certain character types to carry out your story. The story originates from the characters' personality, physical appearance, and emotional life. Just like your life story originates from who you are and how you act, what your goals, hopes, and dreams are, and your physical appearance.

A character's physicality affects the way he feels about himself and how he behaves. Think about the physical type of characters you need for the action in your story, and develop them accordingly. For example, an overweight character may have less self-confidence than a slimmer character, and thus would react differently in given situations. Be sure that your character's actions and reactions are in line with his physical makeup.

The Social

The social aspects of your characters involve everything that pertains to their status and place in society. Did your character go to private school or a neighborhood school? What is her present economic status? Is she wealthy, poor, or middle class? What are her religious beliefs, or is she an atheist? Is she white, African American, Asian? What are her political inclinations? Is she an executive in a Fortune 500 company or does she work in a factory? Does she belong to an expensive fitness center or work out at the local YMCA?

What are your character's hobbies? Does he play tennis, golf, or poker? Does he engage in woodworking, crossword puzzles, or painting? Does he belong to any organizations? What does he do with his leisure time? Is he an intellectual? Is he a social climber or an outcast?

Knowing your characters' social status in relation to society is an absolute necessity. Without knowing their status, you can't determine how they'll be viewed by others or how they view themselves. Think of social novels such as *Babbit* or *Dodsworth* by Sinclair Lewis. In both novels, the main characters are described by their respective social classes.

The Emotional

Although it's important to be familiar with the physical and social traits of your characters in order to help motivate their goals and actions, it doesn't necessarily get to the essence of who your characters are because most physical and social traits are external. To learn about their internal worlds, you must examine the emotional lives of your characters.

The emotional life of your character will determine how he'll act and react in stressful situations. If he feels insecure, he'll behave in a different manner than he would if he were confident. Some of the emotional aspects of your character include self-image. Does he feel depressed about himself, or is he egotistical? What does he fear? Is he able to be in an intimate relationship or does he keep a distance?

What are your character's goals—money, power, or love? Is he an extrovert and the life of the party, or is he an introvert who doesn't trust his feelings to anyone? Is he cynical or sentimental, optimistic or pessimistic? Is he a man's man or a lady's man?

Continue asking and answering more questions along these lines for all three categories. By the time you complete character biographies for all your major characters, your story will be better focused and your characters will have more depth.

When you introduce a character for the first time, what your audience sees is the tip of the iceberg. To avoid creating a trite and one-dimensional character, you need to acknowledge his inner world, his memories, dreams, hopes, and fears. As you slowly reveal information about your character's past, your audience will grow to care about and identify with that character. Your audience also will have empathy for your character if he is presented as a complex and conflicted human being.

Now that you have a solid start on the character, you can make him even more believable by developing a detailed account of his past—what we've referred to earlier as the backstory.

The Backstory

Life can only be understood backwards, but it must be lived forward.—*Søren Kierkegaard*

When I have initial consultations with new clients, I try to better understand who they are in the present by delving into their past. I acquire information about their childhood in order to build a solid case history. For your stories, you'll want to develop a character's backstory, which is similar to a client's case history in therapy. When you begin your story, your characters should already have inner conflicts to resolve and problems to solve.

Creating characters' backstories *before* you start writing is crucial because you'll want to determine each character's past life experiences and the repercussions these experiences will have on your story before you begin. All characters come to your story with a problematic past and unresolved personal conflicts, so you should have a full understanding of what these problems are right from the start—even if your readers don't see the connections until later.

Remember that your characters aren't created in a vacuum; they enter your story with a history, a personality, character traits, and excess baggage, just as you enter relationships with your own past life experiences and your personality traits. You need to make each character's behavior consistent throughout your story, and by fully understanding each character's backstory, you'll be able to achieve this.

Psychological Histories in Backstories

When I develop a case history for a new client, I include a compendium of her character traits, and her psychological disorders or problems, in order to make a diagnosis. Similarly, you can develop a psychological history about your characters to strengthen your backstory.

For example, an individual might come to see me because she's feeling lonely and can't maintain an intimate relationship. But in reality, her problem is that she has low self-esteem and only picks men who are unavailable or unattainable. By exploring her psychology and emotional health, we would work on building up her poor self-image and try to get to the core reason she feels so undeserving.

You will want to develop the psychological and emotional history for your central characters by delving into each character's past and understanding his frame of mind as you work him into your story. When you understand his inner motivations, his actions will become more realistic, and as a result, he'll gain depth.

How do you begin? Well, you learn to ask questions of your characters similar to those I ask of my clients. For example: How did this individual get to be the person she is today? What made her such a caretaker? What type of childhood experiences did she have that still affect her emotionally? What are the beliefs, fears, drives, desires, and basic needs that make up her internal structure? What current self-defeating behavior is directly related to influences from childhood? Do these negative influences come from family, childhood experiences, and teachers? Is she depressed?

Since individuals are the sum total of all their experiences—those

remembered as well as those forgotten—it's important to gather as much information as possible to develop a backstory, including the psychological makeup of your characters.

By continuing to ask relevant questions about their parents, siblings, relatives, memories and life experiences, I discover what makes my clients tick. If their lives are problematic, disappointing, and unfulfilled, I help them gain insight into the root of their self-defeating behaviors and their unrealized desires. As they begin to mine their memories, they find answers to how they've become who they are today.

You need to use the same process of discovery for your characters no matter what genre you're writing. Remember that you are the creator of your characters. You should build layers into their personalities by searching for answers as to why they behave as they do. Don't only concern yourself with what role they play in your story because then you'll only develop surface characters who are stereotypical stick figures. Think of all the clichéd characters you've seen in films or books: the meek librarian, the prostitute with a heart of gold, the grumpy old man, the spinster aunt, the rough but lovable detective. All of these characters have become caricatures because they've been over done.

Once you've developed the proper backstories and psychological profiles for your major characters, you'll need to learn techniques on how to reveal your characters' backstories and psychology throughout your story.

Techniques for Integrating Backstories Into Your Work

The best way to suppose what may come, is to remember what is past.—*Lord Halifax*

In detective stories, you may discover that the next-door neighbor is really a criminal who has killed a lot of people. In a romance, you may learn that the wife really hates her husband and loves his brother.

You might find out that a woman has a reputation as a femme fatale, or a man she loves has been in prison. The most common methods you can use to give the audience such important background information are dialogue, narration, internal dialogue, and flashbacks. These elements provide you with a way to give the audience the necessary information needed to understand the character's past.

Information must be presented in a natural progression and as an integral part of the story, otherwise it will seem forced and unnatural.

Let's look at the different ways you can introduce backstory.

Dialogue

If two people are giving vital information about a character's backstory in a factual conversation, it's likely to be dull and uninteresting to the audience. However, if you show the same two characters having a heated discussion or argument, then the information is revealed through conflict, and it's likely to be more exciting for readers.

Let's say, for example, that a couple is having a conversation at dinner in a restaurant. This is rather uninteresting, unless what they are discussing is highly secretive. The situation becomes even more suspenseful if they are unaware that a man is listening to what they are saying. The audience is aware of the intruder, but the couple isn't and this creates tension. To raise the stakes more, suppose the listener is a spy, hired by a rival to find out the couple's secrets. You're continually creating tension, because the overheard conversation could also endanger the couple's lives.

By constantly making the stakes higher and the conflict greater, you will be able to reveal information and backstory, while simultaneously building more suspense and keeping the action moving.

Tennessee Williams does an excellent job of providing backstory through dialogue in *A Streetcar Named Desire*. When the character Blanche DuBois comes to visit her sister, Stella, and Stella's husband, Stanley Kowalski, at their run-down, cramped apartment, she comes with a suitcase full of secrets. Stanley hates Blanche because he knows she feels superior to him, and as a consequence, he lashes out at Blanche and Stella:

> Who do you think you are? A pair of queens? Now just remember what Huey Long said—that every man's a king—and I'm the king around here, and don't you forget it!

Again, Stanley wants to undermine Blanche to Stella when he reminds her of the good times the two had before Blanche arrived:

> Listen, baby, when we first met—you and me—you thought I was common. Well, how right you was! I was common as dirt. You showed me a snapshot of the place with them columns, and I pulled you down off them columns, and you loved it, having them colored lights goin'! And wasn't we happy together? Wasn't it all OK? Till she showed up here. Hoity-toity, describin' me like an ape.

What colorful, rich dialogue Stanley uses to express his present conflict, while at the same time giving information about his happier past without Blanche!

Narration

Narration is used to tell readers what happened or to provide them with the physical details of events in almost a summary manner.

Let's take a look at an example of narration in action from Alice Sebold's *The Lovely Bones*, in which the narrator, a fourteen-year-old murder victim, kicks off the novel with this:

> My name is Salmon, like the fish; first name, Susie. I was fourteen when I was murdered on December 6, 1973. In news-

paper photos of missing girls from the seventies, most looked like me; white girls with mousy brown hair. This was before kids of all races and genders started appearing on milk cartons or in the daily mail. It was back when people believed things like that didn't happen.

Although it's not done much in modern plays, playwrights used to develop characters who walked directly out of the set or stood in front of the curtain to provide revealing information about the characters to the audience. In Thornton Wilder's Pulitzer Prize-winning *Our Town,* the character of the Stage Manager functions as the narrator when he relates to the audience:

> This is the way we were in our growing-up and in our marrying and in our doctoring and in our living and in our dying.

Another Tennessee Williams play, *The Glass Menagerie,* also makes great use of a narrator. The son, Tom Wingfield, is not only a character in the play, but also the play's narrator.

Inner Dialogue

Thoughts or interior dialogue can also be valuable tools for revealing a character's backstory and psychology. Take a look at this example from Judith Guest's novel *Ordinary People.* Here, we see the central character, Conrad Jarrett, interacting with his swim coach. Notice Conrad's internal thoughts in italics, which ultimately provide readers with far more insight into what the boy's truly feeling and thinking:

> "Jarrett, you got to be kidding me. I don't get it. I excuse you from practice twice a week so you can see some shrink. . . . what the hell more am I supposed to be doing for you?"

"Nothing." *Shrink. Hate that word coarse ignorant just like the kind of word you'd expect from stupid bastard like Salan will not get mad control is all just someday come down here tell him what he can do with his goddamn ignorant opinions.*

Flashbacks

When you interject a scene from the past into the present plot, you're using flashback. Flashbacks are done either visually, as in film, or by using a character's interior thoughts or interior monologue, as in prose. The flashback gives information or an explanation about a specific character or event that is important for the audience to know. Be careful, however, not to use a flashback if it has no relationship to the present scene you're writing or if it will create confusion. Flashbacks can often slow down a story or interrupt the flow, so you'll want to make sure you weave them in smoothly.

Toward the end of F. Scott Fitzgerald's *The Great Gatsby*, the narrator of the novel, Nick Carraway, relates through summary Gatsby's last night with Daisy before Gatsby goes off to war:

On the last afternoon before he went abroad, he sat with Daisy in his arms for a long, silent time. It was a cold fall day, with fire in the room and her cheeks flushed. Now and then she moved and he changed his arm a little, and once he kissed her dark shining hair. The afternoon had made them tranquil for a while, as if to give them a deep memory for the long parting the next day promised. They had never been closer in their month of love, nor communicated more profoundly one with another, than when she brushed silent lips against his coat's shoulder or when he touched the end of her fingers, gently, as though she were asleep.

This flashback, one of many in the novel, not only provides readers with a glimpse of the relationship Gatsby and Daisy once shared, but

also adds emphasis to angst now felt by Gatsby as he watches Daisy
with her husband, Tom.

Remember that you want a flashback to enhance your present
story and allow the audience to learn secrets from the past, so they'll
understand what's happening. However, if you're going to include
flashbacks, don't rely on them to structure your story, and make sure
you use them sparingly.

Transactional Analysis

Now that you've explored your own past, as well as that of your
characters, it's time to focus on melding those experiences and emotions in order to add originality and depth to your characters. You
can write more easily by reconnecting to the free child inside you and
the ones inside your characters by using transactional analysis.

Transactional analysis was developed by Eric Berne, a well-known
psychiatrist and medical doctor. Transactional analysis is a theory of
personality that identifies three separate ego states: the parent, the child,
and the adult. From his observations of therapy patients, Berne believed
that every individual operates from these three ego states at any given
time. He also stated that there are two components to the child ego
state. The first component is the free child and the other is the adapted
child.

The Free Child

**The secret of genius is to carry the spirit of the child into old
age, which means never losing your enthusiasm.**
—*Aldous Huxley*

By learning to tap into your free child, you'll be able to give your
characters increased spontaneity and depth. The free child is spontaneous, outgoing, creative, playful, and autonomous. In Berne's book
Games People Play, he states, "Each person carries around within him-

self a little boy or a little girl, who feels, thinks, acts, talks, and responds just the way he or she did when he or she was a child of a certain age."

When you first begin to create your characters, allow that spontaneous, playful side of yourself to emerge through them. Become courageous, and don't be afraid to let go; have fun with your writing and let wonderment show through your characters. Don't let your inner critic interfere with your free child.

To write rich characters who are unique and filled with contradictions and complexities, you need to have the courage to return to your childhood memories, to a place where you were freer and less self-conscious. The way to give life to your characters is to reexperience your spontaneous, intuitive side and let it emerge through your characters.

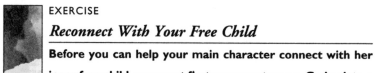

EXERCISE

Reconnect With Your Free Child

Before you can help your main character connect with her inner free child, you must first reconnect yours. Go back to a time in childhood when you recall your free child side doing something spontaneous or creative. Relive the scene with all of your senses and reexperience it emotionally. How does it feel to be free, natural, and courageous? Write down the details, colors, smells, sounds, sights, and textures of where you are and what you're doing. Maybe you are drawing a picture, singing a song, dancing at a recital, or just playing in the sand. Keep writing for twenty minutes. When you are finished, read what you've written aloud.

How do you feel now that you've reconnected to part of your free child? What's the sensation of feeling natural and free? Exhilarating? Emotional? Exhausting? Try to awaken your free child every time you start to write, and you will be surprised at how original and exciting the characters you create will be. After you've completed

the exercises for yourself, do them for your characters, so that
you'll have more insight into them. ▪ ▪ ▪   35

The Adapted Child

> No person is your friend who demands your silence, or denies
> your right to grow.—*Alice Walker*

The other child ego state Berne refers to is the adapted child, the one
who has learned to adapt himself in order to survive. The adapted
child worries about people liking him and tries to please everyone.
He has lost all the wonderful qualities of the free child and becomes
compliant, fearful, guilty, and cautious. The adapted child believes
the best possible way to get along is to conform to his parents' rules
and regulations. But the more he conforms, the more he loses the
joyful qualities of the free child.

I have consulted with all types of writers, from beginners to award-
winning professionals, who became too concerned with the results of
their writing before they had ever written anything. Their negative
inner dialogue was: "Will it be good?" "How much will I be paid?"
"I have nothing to say." "I can't create good characters." "My writing
is terrible." "You can't make a living as a writer."

These judgmental attitudes crippled them until they weren't able
to write at all. They became blocked because their adapted child took
over and their free child was silenced. Only when they did the following exercise were they able to begin to free themselves of all their
internal criticisms from the ghosts of the past. By learning to silence
their inner critics, these writers were able to free themselves from self-
censorship and create layered and uninhibited characters.

EXERCISE

Connecting With Your Inner Critic

Close your eyes and think back to a time when you encoun-
tered negative feedback. Visualize the incident and listen to

words. Now, as quickly as you can, write down the negative messages you hear. Who's saying them? Your father or mother? A teacher? A boss?

After you identify the original messenger, change your negative thinking by writing positive messages that counteract the negative ones. This will enable you to eventually let go of your own inner critic and silence the part of you that still believes what you were told as a young child.

The inner critic makes it difficult for many writers to be playful, courageous, and joyful when they first start to create characters. They still hear their parents' critical voices communicating negative messages to them, and they become timid and self-conscious with their creativity. Read the positive messages that counteract your negative ones for as long as it takes to silence the criticism.

Remember, your fictional characters have negative messages inside them, too. It's up to you to discover their internal negative judgments and help your characters revise negative thoughts to positive ones, just as you've done for yourself. This will enable your fictional characters to have a transformation by the end of your story. You can achieve this by presenting your characters with a problem. Maybe they are fearful or have low self-esteem stemming from their childhood. By having them overcome obstacles in the plot and, at the same time, overcome their negative feelings, your characters will eventually experience an emotional transformation.

By getting in touch with your free child and changing your negative inner dialogue to positive inner dialogue, you'll write from a more intuitive and spontaneous place. As you have a better understanding of your own backstory and your character's backstory, you'll both eventually be free from the ghosts of the past. ■ ■ ■

pulling the strings: character motivation

Writing is an exploration. You start from nothing and learn as you go. —*E.L. Doctorow*

ood character development is impossible without sound motivation. In order to create successful characters you must make sense of their actions and behavior. You need to know about your characters' past in order to understand what motivates them in the present. But what is a motive? A motive is a need or desire that makes a person take action. Motives may be conscious or unconscious, and each character may respond to the same motive, such as hunger, in different ways.

Motivation is the cause or moving force behind all the conflict, action, and turmoil your characters experience in a story. Without motivating your characters' actions, your characters will fail because their behavior won't make sense.

Unfortunately, many writers don't know how to motivate the characters in their stories. They concentrate only on plot, and, as a result, their stories are filled with characters whose actions and reactions are implausible, inconsistent, and unbelievable. It doesn't matter how well the story is structured. If the characters aren't believable, the plot won't work. Even the greatest story will collapse under the weight of unmotivated characters.

For example, if you're reading a book about a shy, retiring character who suddenly changes without any reason into an outgoing, aggres-

37

sive, forceful individual, you certainly wouldn't be convinced of the character's dramatic transformation. That's because the motivation is missing and his actions would be "out of character." From that point on, the writer has lost you and the story is no longer working.

Motivating a Main Character: A Scenario

Motivation comes from within. —*Anonymous*

The following example and accompanying exercise show you how to approach character motivation. The scenario also demonstrates the necessary steps for successfully motivating your character and shaping your story's plot, while simultaneously illustrating how important it is that your character's choices, actions, and reactions remain consistent with her personality. Pay attention, because you'll be doing this with your characters through a similar scenario next!

Suzi Dove is twenty-nine and has never really dated because she is overweight and very introverted. She has told her friends and family that she's perfectly okay with the way she looks and being fat doesn't bother her. When she takes a new job as an executive assistant to the CEO of a technical corporation, she secretly becomes attracted to Tom, a computer programmer in the company. She is surprised when he pays attention to her, asking her questions about herself and showing an interest in her during their coffee break.

For the first time in her adult life, an attractive man has shown her attention. Suzi's not used to it and doesn't know how to react. But as she gets more comfortable she allows herself to fantasize that one day Tom may ask her out on a date. But she thinks it's impossible because he dates many beautiful women and why would he want to date a woman fifty pounds overweight?

Internal and External Motivation

Even though Suzi has acted as if her weight didn't bother her, in truth, it has left her feeling ashamed of her body and unattractive. Deep inside she feels insecure and blames herself for being weak. Her attraction to Tom grows in spite of her insecurity. She never before had romantic feelings and for the first time she is determined to lose weight. Her change of attitude about her weight has been motivated by her strong feelings toward Tom. Wanting love is an *internal* need she must satisfy. Without her internal motivation she wouldn't have a clear external goal. Thus, her *external* need is to lose weight in the hope that Tom with ask her for a date. The goal of her story (the external problem that needs to be solved) is now her desire to get a date with Tom. It is the impetus that drives the story and plot forward.

Upping the Stakes

Simply giving Suzi a specific goal is not enough to move the story, because we also have to up the stakes to keep the reader's attention. To give the story more tension, try this scenario: A co-worker who knows Suzi has a crush on Tom challenges her to lose weight in order to get a date with Tom. When she accepts the dare, her co-worker challenges her again, this time to accomplish her goal before reaching her thirtieth birthday, which is only three months away. And what if her friend ups the stakes even more by making a monetary bet that says Suzi will have to lose a specific number of pounds or pay her five hundred dollars if Tom doesn't ask her out before her birthday.

By giving Suzi a time limit in which to lose a specific amount of weight to reach her goal and by putting into place potential conse-quences if she fails, we've given her a much stronger motivation for her actions.

Suzi takes immediate action and cuts sweets from her diet. After one month, she has lost fifteen pounds and her clothes are a little loose. She feels more motivated, and she also stops eating bread and potatoes. She decides that she has to exercise. Since she feels too ashamed of her body to join a fitness center, she begins to get off the bus at an earlier stop, increasing the number of blocks she needs to walk to work. After time, she skips the bus completely and walks the entire ten blocks.

Although her motivation was external—to lose weight in order to be more attractive to Tom so he would ask her out—she inadvertently has changed her internal needs.

Suzi is now feeling better about herself, and as she loses weight, her self-confidence increases. Her weight loss also affects her self-image. With the help of her best friend, she buys new fitted clothes in place of her baggier outfits. People at work begin to notice her slim figure and compliment her on how good she looks.

As she loses weight and feels better about herself, she increases her confidence by going for a complete makeover and a flattering new hair style. She keeps losing weight, and soon she joins a health club and begins to shape up her body. This is the very first time she has ever viewed herself as being feminine. Her entire self-image is transforming from negative to positive.

Suddenly men at the office and at the health club begin to notice her. As she receives more and more attention from the opposite sex, her personality blossoms. She starts to date and, before her thirtieth birthday, Tom asks her out. After dating for a couple of months, the two fall deeply in love and get married. She is a beautiful, thin, confident bride.

Your story's action springs from the character's struggle to reach her external motivation. It defines the answer to the dramatic ques-

tion: "What does the character want in this story?" The above example
was fairly straight forward and linear.

Suzi's complete physical transformation enabled her to discover
insights about herself. Reaching her external goal also transformed
Suzi's internal structure. She went from feeling shame, which she
denied, to feeling self-esteem; from a lack of confidence to feeling
confident; and from being disgusted by her body to being proud
of it.

EXERCISE

Motivating Your *Main Character*

Now that you've seen how character development and motivation are interconnected, complete the following exercise
for your own story. Work with your characters and develop the necessary external and internal motivation for them. This takes a lot of
thought and planning because you need to discover the correct motivation for your story's plot and your main character's goal.

You'll want to develop an internal need or drive for all of your characters. Even if they aren't consciously aware of what their internal needs
are, you must know. Build a solid foundation for your characters so they
won't fall apart halfway through your work. Before you begin to develop
their motivation, you may need to ask yourself more questions about
each character's past life experiences: Where did she come from? Why
does she behave the way she does? What was her childhood like? How
did she relate to her classmates? Did she have a lot of boyfriends? Was
she good in sports? Knowing the answers to these questions and others,
will give your characters more dimension and complexity.

Were you successful in completing this exercise for your characters? Do you see how the external problem creates the action your
main character needs to take throughout the story? Are you characters internally motivated as well? Do you now know how they will
grow and change throughout your story? ▪ ▪ ▪

Character Motivation Based on Backstory

Writers are the main landmarks of the past.

—*Edward G. Bulwer-Lytton*

As we learned in chapter two, your characters always come to your present story with a backstory. Backstory can dramatically affect your character's present behavior and motivation.

Let's continue with the previous example about Suzi. By including her backstory, you'll see how she will have more conflicts:

For most of her life, Suzi desperately wanted to be thin but always had a weight problem. As a young child who was lonely and shy, she used food to soothe her sadness. Food was her comfort, her solace against ridicule about her weight when kids laughed at her. In elementary school, the kids made fun of her on the playground. In high school, she sat alone eating pizza and ice cream, while her classmates were out at all-night prom parties.

Her coping skills developed by turning to food no matter what the circumstances, and she continued to gain in spite of her mother's nagging and her father's ridicule. She became a sneak eater, hiding her stash of food. Although she tried hundreds of diets, she would eventually gain back whatever she'd lost. Frustrated with all of her failures, she decided that she no longer cared about losing weight. So she stopped her "yo-yo" diets and accepted the fact that she was going to be big and beautiful all her life. (But not really.)

Her best friends were attractive, thin girls who eventually married. She always attended their weddings but was never close to being married herself. The most painful insult she'd suffered was when her best friend told her that she was sorry, but that Suzi was too heavy to fit into the bridesmaid's gown. Suzi never recovered from that humiliating experience, although she didn't let her friend see how hurt she was.

By knowing Suzi's backstory, you can see the conflict increase. Suzi is now quite a different character than the one portrayed in the earlier scenario. Her backstory provides the basis for her more internal conflicts, poorer coping skills, and her constant struggle with her weight. Using this information from her past helps to create more conflict between her internal goal—love—and her external goal—Tom.

Consider this alternative: Maybe Suzi struggles to lose weight, but, in the end, her desire to satisfy her insecurity through eating is stronger than her desire to win Tom's love. Remember, it's important that your character *struggle* toward her goal, but she doesn't need to necessarily attain the goal.

Now, continue with the exercise you started on page 41. Give your characters inner and outer goals, while concentrating on how their past and their psychology affects their present motivation. How are they a victim of past behavior? Do they have such low self-esteem from their childhood that they don't believe they can change? Are they afraid to struggle to attain their goal? Is their present motivation strong enough to overcome their past struggles? As you keep combining the characters' past with their inner and outer problems, you will be creating more emotional characters with inner depth.

When you create a character, be certain to give him a *specific* goal that properly sets up the motivation for him to take action and move the story forward. Decide right now what story you want to write, and use that as the main character's external motivation. For example, maybe your character wants love. Well, it has to be the love of a specific person. Or, let's say your character wants power. The goal should be specific and clear to readers so that they can cheer the main character on as he struggles to achieve it.

CAUSAL WRITING

Writing is nothing more than a guided dream.

—Jorge Luis Borges

Causal writing is used in all genres of writing, because the beginning of your story must relate to the end. This means that each chapter or scene you write should come from the one before it and cause the chapter or scene following it. That's why it's referred to as causal writing, because the chapters and scenes must be connected to one another from beginning to the end.

Think of your writing as connected, one word to the next and one page after the other, just like a setup of dominos. When you hit the first domino the entire structure will start falling and move right down to the very last piece because they are all connected.

You can't motivate your characters if your writing is not causal. Their motivations, just like your writing, must cause the next action and then the next. One external action causes another action. Causal writing keeps the characters' actions focused toward the climax of the story.

After you've determined the external motivation for your main character, see how it makes your story more direct. Doesn't your character's goal seem more focused and clear? It should be, and if it's not, you'll need to work on your character's external motivation until it drives his actions directly toward his goal. ✧

Needs and Motivation

I saw the angel in the marble and carved until I set him free.

—*Michelangelo*

You can see that your character's internal motivation is much less obvious than the external goal and often unknown to the character herself. You could say her inner need is in her unconscious, of which she is unaware. However, you need to be aware of it, and you need to answer the most important question for all your characters and their motivations: "Why?"

"Why is my character going to kill his mother?" "Why does my character want to be an actress?" "Why is my hero fearful?" "Why is my antagonist so vicious?"

The "why" is your character's motivation, what makes her tick.

There are many different theories on motivation—some have to do with the internal needs of the individual, such as satisfying inner needs like hunger or love. Other needs are external, such as the need for attention or the need for affiliation with a group. One theory on motivation suggests that man does the things he does because of his needs, and he takes direct action to satisfy them. Since the needs of human beings are considered the source of motivation, the strongest need is the need that determines their actions. At that time the most pressing need takes precedence over the other needs.

According to behavioral scientist Abraham Maslow, these needs motivate human actions only as long as the needs are not satisfied. Once a need is satisfied, it no longer motivates. In "A Theory of Human Motivation," Maslow wrote, "For the man who is extremely and dangerously hungry, no other interest exists but food. He dreams of food, he remembers food, he thinks about food, he emotes about food, he perceives only food and he wants only food."

These needs, to which man's actions are directed, can be categorized and compared in their relative importance as they influence man's actions. Maslow arranged these needs in a hierarchy as indicated below. When a need at any one level is satisfied, the next level need becomes predominant. By studying Maslow's hierarchy of needs, you will learn different degrees of your characters' drives and find the best motivation for your characters.

1. **Physiological Needs:** As indicated in the hierarchy, the first level need is the basic human need related to the sustenance of life itself,

such as food, clothing, and shelter. Once the physiological needs become satisfied the person goes on to the next level.

2. **Safety and Security Needs:** The next level need, safety and security, becomes the predominant motivator. This level is equivalent to the need for self-preservation. It is not only the need to be free from physical endangerment, but also the perception that this is so. It is primarily a physiological need.

3. **Affiliation Needs:** The next level need is affiliation or belonging, which emerges as the dominant need. It is the need to share a physical closeness with others, along with a need for acceptance by the group, and is the first sociological need.

4. **Esteem Needs:** Once the affiliation need is satisfied, esteem becomes dominant. This is the need for the individual to be recognized by the group as being outstanding for some reason, as well as the need for self-esteem which is based on the recognition of others.

5. **Self-Actualization Needs:** Once esteem needs have been satisfied, the need for self-actualization becomes more dominant as the motivator. Self-actualization has to do with the individual's concepts of life and those things that each individual feels are needed to maximize one's potential, whatever it may be. You know you are self-actualized when you're doing or accomplishing those things in your life that you feel you should be doing.

Knowledge of the Maslow's hierarchy of needs can help you identify motivation for all of your characters. Every one of your characters will vary widely as to where he is in the hierarchy. Many characters will move to different levels of needs after they have satisfied the previous need. Just remember that your characters, as human beings, will act in specific ways because of the dominant need that influences their behavior at the time.

For example, by using the most basic needs for your fictional characters, you'll give them a greater degree of motivation for sustenance or survival. Think of all the books and films based on survival such as *The Mosquito Coast, Lord of the Flies,* or even *Jaws.* Survival needs create the most tension and suspense in a story. If your character is on a desert island craving water, she isn't going to be thinking about satisfying her creativity.

Can you recall some of the stories you've read or films you've seen where the characters' lives are threatened by lack of food or water? *Alive,* by Piers Paul Read, recounts the true tale of a plane carrying members of a rugby team who were traveling from Uruguay to Chile for a match, crashed in a desolate part of the Andes mountains. Of the forty-five passengers and crew who started the trip, only sixteen survived and were left stranded in the snowcapped mountains with no food, water, or shelter. They eventually committed one of the most horrific acts of brutality—they cannibalized their fellow members who had died!

This was an unimaginable act to these men, and one that they probably never dreamed possible for them to commit. However, under the right circumstances, anyone can commit the unimaginable if given strong enough motivation to survive the elements or life threatening circumstances.

You can motivate your characters to do anything, especially if their survival depends on it. Take the most basic physiological needs of your characters and motivate them to commit an extraordinary action to satisfy that need. Write a life-or-death situation for your character and motivate his behavior so it is believable and realistic.

Emotions and Motivation

A belief that does not spring from a conviction in the emotions is no belief at all. —*Evelyn Scott*

Remember that motivation always springs from an emotional need, whether it's the need for love, revenge, power, desire, fame, respect, survival, or recognition. Before you create your characters from the inside, you need to reach inside yourself to discover what motivates your own behaviors. When you write, you need to become introspective and discover those forces inside you that motivate your actions.

Ask the same questions of yourself before you ask them of your characters. From what inner needs do your motivations bubble up? What external motivations determine your life, career, and relationship goals? Have you been able to satisfy your needs? Which ones have you struggled to attain? What inner conflicts prevent you from reaching your goals?

Answer these questions of yourself, and then ask the same questions of your characters. Put your own feelings, needs, and desires into your fictional characters to build realistic and consistent characters, whose actions are coherent and believable. Whenever you start a new story go inward and pull your feelings to the surface. By considering your feelings and motivating your characters before your write, you'll have complex and emotional human beings whom your readers will root for and believe in no matter how fantastic the story.

less of you: creating characters different from yourself

I was always looking outside myself for strength and confidence but it comes from within. It was there all the time.
—*Anna Freud*

*M*any writers often believe that everyone is interested in
their personal lives, and so they naturally want to write
about their latest breakup or romance. Unfortunately these are often the last things readers want from a novel. Why? Because readers
and viewers want to be entertained by fiction, to be suspended in
disbelief and to be involved in a story that takes them outside of
their own realities.

As a therapist, I believe that writers who write themselves into their
own stories are doing so to make sense of their lives. You don't choose
your writing subject by accident, especially if it's based on a personal
life experience. Those newer to the craft may write the story of "Why
my mother liked my brother better than me," or "Why my father
didn't have time to be a father, because he was too busy working."
In other words, they write about an aspect of their own life story,
which is important and interesting to them, but which may bore
audiences.

This type of writing works if you're planning on writing your
autobiography or memoir, but it doesn't work if you're writing
fictional stories. With fiction, you need to structure a story that is
exciting and filled with three-dimensional characters. The obliga-

tion of good fiction is to entertain your readers and hold their interest by creating characters who are different from yourself and by turning your personal story into one that is dramatic and dynamic.

In this chapter, you will learn how to do just that—to take your personal life story and transform it into a powerful fictional story with fully developed characters living in an exciting plot.

Consider the following: Can you take what happened to you and turn it into an exciting story with a beginning, middle, and end? Can you create characters for your story who have a goal and overcome obstacles along the way? Can you give your story a main character who will finally reach her goal and have an emotional transformation or change in the climax? If you answer "yes," to all three questions then you are well on the road to writing characters different from yourself.

Less of You

Do I contradict myself? Very well, then, I contradict myself,
(I am large, I contain multitudes). —*Walt Whitman*

When you write fiction you must use your life experience and knowledge of craft—character, dialogue, theme, conflict, structure—to transform your experience into fiction that is professionally written.

You might wonder why so many writing instructors tell you to write what you know and yet, when you do, they say it's not working because there's too much of you in the story. Well, since you create the characters and the plot, you're creating a universe. You're playing God by creating a world with rules and human beings who are going on a journey. You need to use yourself as the creative source from which you'll write your story because you are the only person with your unique abilities. You'll need to draw upon your life experiences, your emotional world, and your own psychology to make your story fresh and original. At this moment you have hundreds of stories inside of you, enough to write for a lifetime. After all, there is nobody else in the world exactly like you, and nobody but you can write the story you want to tell. However, that doesn't mean you should write exactly what happened.

Neil Simon has enjoyed tremendous success with his two autobiographical plays, *Broadway Bound* and *Brighton Beach Memoirs*, in which he used characters from his childhood. But his genius was in taking real life and making it more humorous and heartfelt than common reality is usually capable of providing on its own. In your writing, it's imperative to recognize the fragile dance you need to perform in order to put parts of yourself into your characters, while at the same time, creating characters who are unique and different from you. "How can I accomplish this?" you may ask. "First you tell me to create characters different from myself and then you tell me to put parts of myself into the characters. Isn't that a contradiction?" Yes, it is a contradiction, but it is one all writers must face.

Writing about real people and real life is a great jumping-off point for creating fictional characters who are dynamic and believable. So, it's not really a contradiction, because people and incidents from your life are the motivation and the impetus for you to create a story that is important to you. You shouldn't write any story unless it has meaning to you. Most of the best scripts and novels are those that came from a significant aspect of the writer's life, even if it was just a moment in time or a fragment of an experience.

Truman Capote's touching short story "A Christmas Memory" was based on his childhood memory of his last Christmas with his older cousin. The story tells of a close bond between the two cousins, an older woman, and a young boy, and how they share their last Christmas together. It was later turned into a television program that still airs during the Christmas season because of its universal theme of emotional closeness and love.

EXERCISE
Personal Transformations

Take a heartfelt memory from your childhood, such as a holiday memory or an incident that you recall with a favorite
relative. Using your senses of touch, taste, sound, sight, and smell,
write for about fifteen to twenty minutes as fast as you can without
stopping. After you have completed the exercise, use what you wrote
as the basis for a fictional character in a story. That means you can
use the feelings that touched your heart, but now you need to put
them into a character and write a story with a beginning, middle, and
end.

By writing this way you're allowing your right brain to visualize the
memories. After you do the freewriting, you can use your left brain
to organize the material and to shape your characters into fiction.
The beauty of this type of writing is that you are first able to get the
story down without censoring yourself.

When you create characters and write a personal story, you may
be unconsciously working through some unfinished business of your
life. The wonderful result may be that you experience a personal
transformation just as your main character experiences a transformational arc in the story. This can be an exciting opportunity for self-
discovery on a personal level, and it enables you to create a touching,
heartfelt story and to reveal your truth. ■ ■ ■

Your Inner Characters

> It is only with the heart that one can see rightly; what is essen-
> tial is invisible to the eye. —*Antoine de Saint-Exupery*

Your inner characters reside inside you. They're those parts of you
that are contradictory and complementary, those selves that are opposites and polarizing. These divergent parts of your personality often
create the biggest resistance to change and risk taking. If you want to

meet your worst enemy and your best friend—just look in the mirror at yourself. The same goes for your characters.   **53**

By going on an inner journey you'll discover the most important resources needed to create characters filled with internal struggles just like you. Writing from parts of yourself will allow your characters to grow and change as they go through their journey. We tend to compartmentalize parts of our personality. Thus we have many selves that are never exposed or expressed to others, or even to ourselves. Our dreams and fantasies often reveal these hidden parts of ourselves. We also switch selves depending on our environment: You don't act the same at work as you do at home. You treat your father different from your mother, teachers different from peers, friends different from foes, lovers different from siblings.

We have many parts to our personality that are disparate and diversified. These aspects of our personality often make us at odds with others as well as ourselves. Your characters also need to have many contradicting personalities and selves to make them interesting and complex. You'll soon discover how these contradictions make sense, and you'll be able to use them to give your characters greater depth. As you accept the fact that you contradict yourself, you'll be able to create more diverse, flesh and blood characters.

EXERCISE
Identifying Your Inner Characters

Write down the different inner characters that live inside of you. For example you might include: the inner critic, the good little girl, the wise self, etc. Make a list and try to get at least ten to twenty inner characters who you can draw upon when creating your characters. After you have written this list, create a list for your main characters. Who are their inner characters and how do they affect their behavior in your story? Do their inner selves give them more complexity? Do they behave and react differently with other

characters? Do they have a thread of inner strength to draw upon in times of danger? How do your characters differ from one another? How do they solve their problems by using their inner characters? ■ ■ ■

The exercise you just completed will help you get in touch with parts of your personality that have been dormant or hidden away. Many writers only write from one voice—usually the victim's voice, thus only showing readers a character who is helpless and dependent on others. Inside, there are many personalities you need to call upon when writing stories of stronger characters. For example, women writers may have trouble connecting to their animus, which, according to Carl Jung, is the masculine side of their personality. It is important for women to connect to their animus when writing a story with a strong or aggressive character. Mystery writer Elizabeth George stresses the psychological profile and family history of her characters, and was able to get in touch with her animus when she created her detective, Scotland Yard Inspector, Thomas Lynley, the eighth Earl of Asherton in her first novel *A Great Deliverance.*

Just as a woman writer needs to reach her animus, a man needs to get in touch with his anima, the feminine side of himself, especially when writing about characters who are emotionally expressive and giving. Tennessee Williams, the famous playwright, certainly succeeded in creating female characters who were giving, sensitive, and vulnerable such as Blanche DuBois in *A Streetcar Named Desire* and Laura Wingfield in *The Glass Menagerie,* by tapping into his anima.

Like male and female writers, characters also need to connect with their feminine and masculine sides. A writer capable of connecting with his or her own anima or animus will find it much easier to create such complex characters than a writer who is limited to his or her own perspective.

Method Writing

Write from experience and experience only. Try to be one of
the people on whom nothing is lost. —*Henry James*

Famous actors such as Robert De Niro and Al Pacino prepare for
their roles through a process called method acting, taught by the
highly respected acting teacher Lee Strasberg. Method acting requires
actors to go inside themselves to recall their feelings, sensory memories, affective or emotional memories, concentration, focus, and emotions. Similarly, good writers must also prepare themselves in advance
for developing their fictional characters by going inside themselves.
Just as there is method acting, I would like to propose method writing
as a way for you to delve deeper into your characters, making them
different from yourself.

To engage in method writing, you need to target a sensory memory
from the past in which you felt emotions similar to those that you
want your fictional character to experience. By tapping into your
memory with all of your senses, you will retrieve these emotions,
which are always with you, but not available without relaxation and
visualization.

The longer I teach writing, the more I've come to believe that
method writing is just as important, if not more so, for writers to
learn as traditional writing methods. It is the writers who are the
creators of all the characters in a story, film, or play. To prepare for
their roles, actors ask in-depth questions of their characters such as:
"What does my character want?" "What context or background does
my character come from?" "What is the emotional makeup of my
character?" "Does my character have high self-esteem or is he suffering
from low self-worth?" These questions help method actors find meaning in a role.

Doesn't it make sense for you, the writer, to be asking the same
questions of your characters *before* you create them? After all, you're

creating a world filled with human beings who all have hopes and desires, needs and wants, fears and dreams—similar to the ones you have.

With method writing, you must also do the necessary research to learn about aspects of your characters that you are less familiar with. How does a boxer train? What does a stripper do to become a stripper? How do the homeless live? How do criminals commit their crimes? It is important for you to put yourself in your characters' shoes in order to feel and think like the characters. By doing your research and putting your emotions into your characters, you will be able to give them greater emotional depth.

EXERCISE

Recalling Sensory Memories

Get in touch with your own sensory memory as you recall a real person in your life with whom you had an emotional relationship. Close your eyes and try to remember your emotions at the time. Were you in love? Did you argue? What was the most prominent emotion you felt? Now using all of your senses, write about the relationship and your feelings about it. Don't stop writing for at least fifteen minutes. Immerse yourself in the scene. After you've written about the relationship, put your personal emotions into a fictional character by using method writing to recover your feelings. ■ ■ ■

The Writer as All the Characters

> **Every human being has hundreds of separate people living under his skin.** —*Mel Brooks*

In the early 1990s, I developed a course at UCLA writer's program titled "The Writer as All the Characters." It quickly filled with all types of writers, even those writing nonfiction. Many were curious about the title and couldn't wait to learn how they could become all the characters. Some were resistant to the fact that they were all the characters because they didn't want to admit that any of the undesirable traits in their characters were also in them.

Well, it's true. You, the writer, are all the characters. Without your imagination, life experiences, and internal world you wouldn't be able to develop diverse characters. If you are able to access your various selves and put those aspects of yourself into your characters, regardless of whether you have actually experienced the same situation, you'll create great characters for every story you write. As the writer of all the characters in a story, you should be able to discover reasons for their internal needs and drives. If you are unable to do this, your characters will feel flat, forced, and fake.

As we discussed earlier, Jung believed we have a collective unconscious where archetypes or universal characters reside. The following is a list of some of these archetypal characters:

Wise old man/woman: has living experiences that incorporate inner wisdom

Little professor: intelligent, mature child who pleases parents by getting good grades

Perfect child: does everything right and always obeys

Femme fatale: sexpot, vixen, siren

Hunk: a macho stud, Don Juan, a sexy lady's man

Amazon woman: capable, independent, self-sufficient

Witch/bitch: overly aggressive, cold

Wallflower: shy, insecure, stays in background

Dictator: pushes and prods others into doing things they don't want to do, domineering and overly controlling

Rebel: nonconformist, stubborn, rule-breaker, goes against the grain

Big shot: wealthy, insistent, overconcerned with one's own reputation

Madonna: mother figure, caretaker, revered and respected

Victim: waits to be taken care of, wants to be rescued, "poor me" approach to life

Little prince/princess: spoiled, demanding, wants to be waited on by others

People-pleaser: wants to make others happy, needs constant approval from others

Joker, prankster, clown: entertainer, plays practical jokes, mischievous

Perfectionist: desires to have everything "just right," always training to do better

Warrior: saves the day, fights off the enemies, strong

Rescuer: saves others from peril or even from themselves if need be

Pygmalion: tries to change or "make over" others into something else

Martyr: willing to sacrifice one's life for the sake of others, for the "greater good"

Critic: never fully satisfied, always has something negative to say

Judge: judges, censors, and evaluates others

Vulnerable little child: defenseless, easily preyed-upon victim

Try to find the archetypes inside yourself, where all your emotions and feelings are collected. Open yourself to all of them—the good and the bad. As you'll discover in the exercise below, when you reconnect with your archetypes, you'll create powerful visual images and dynamic, universal characters and stories.

EXERCISE
You, Your Archetypes, and Your Characters

Read over the list and see how many of these archetypes you can identify in yourself. Keep in mind that while archetypes are similar to the inner characters we discussed on page 52, they are,

in actuality, far more universal. Now take your archetypes and put
them in some of your fictional characters. Choose one or two qualities   59
of your particular archetypes for each of your characters in your story
and use these archetypes in order to make him or her come alive.

Whether the characters you create are heroes or heroines, villains
or vixens, Madonnas or martyrs, they are based on these universal
archetypes. By connecting to your archetypes and employing them in
your story you'll create powerful, dynamic characters who touch the
collective unconscious of your audience. ■ ■ ■

If you are able to write from your personal experiences and transform them into powerful fictional characters and stories, you'll have
succeeded as a writer. Writers often ask me, "How can I write about
being a beauty queen if I've never been one?" "How can I write about
being a prisoner if I've never been in jail?"

Well, you can. That's why you're a writer—use your imagination
and creativity to go inside yourself. Access those parts of you that
know what it feels to be attractive, or know the feeling of being
trapped or caged. You aren't limited to only writing what you know.
You also want to write what you feel.

Reach inside yourself and put your romantic feelings into your
characters who fall in love, like William Shakespeare did in *Romeo
and Juliet.* When Margaret Mitchell wrote *Gone with the Wind,* she
created larger than life romantic characters, Scarlett O'Hara and Rhett
Butler.

If you can develop characters who emulate the passion of Scarlett
and Rhett, your characters will come alive. Take your loving feelings
and put them into a romance between your fictional characters, one
that your readers root for, hoping that the characters will get together
in the end. Even if you're not a mother, father, murderer, preacher,
cheerleader, or beauty queen, you can still write about these characters
by connecting with all the various human beings residing inside you.

As a writer who knows the importance of reaching deep inside to access your emotions, feelings, and memories, you have enough stories inside you to last a lifetime. The secret is to take your life experiences, your psychology, and your emotional world, and put them into fictional characters. You don't have to be a lover boy to be romantic, and you don't have to be a femme fatale to attract a man. Conversely, you don't have to be a husband and father to create characters who are family men, and you don't have to be a spinster to know about loneliness and isolation.

However, you must get emotional distance from real life situations or real people before you try to write about them. Recently, a writer consulted with me about writing a story about her husband's death. She was in the middle of mourning and still very distraught about his unexpected death. I explained that it would be helpful if she wrote in her journal about her feelings, pain, and despair, but that she should wait until more time passed—until she was no longer living in the throes of her pain—before working his story into a novel. At first she didn't understand what I meant, but when I explained she was too close to the incident to be objective, she understood.

If you have a person from your life who you want to write about, make certain enough time has elapsed so that you can approach him or her with an objective writer's eye and have enough distance to be able to create a composite character to tell your story, otherwise you will be too subjective and won't be able to successfully create a fictional character who works.

From Real People to Fictional Characters

The writer isn't made in a vacuum. Writers are witnesses.

—*E.L. Doctorow*

Many things happen in life that don't necessarily make for good fiction. For example, in fiction, characters shouldn't meet or have things happen to them through coincidence because such occurrences can lack realism. Instead, the characters need to be motivated and there has to be a basis for what happens to them. Yet, in life, coincidences can and do happen all the time, which accounts for the saying, "Life is stranger than fiction."

In life, people can be boring and dialogue can often be filled with grunts, "ahs" and "ehs." In fiction, dialogue must give information to move the story forward and reveal the character in some way. If the dialogue doesn't accomplish this in a work of fiction, you risk losing the reader's attention.

You need to create characters who hold your readers' interest and who tell a good story—that's what matters. In many instances, writers are afraid to write about a particular person from their life, especially if their character isn't a nice or sympathetic one. While you'll want to take some cautions, such as changing the character's profession or gender, you shouldn't worry too much. In my experience, I've discovered that the nastiest, most mean-spirited people don't usually think of themselves in that way. Most people believe they're pleasant and that everyone else is a problem. Odds are, they probably wouldn't even realize they're the inspiration for that miserable cad or mean scoundrel in your story. So don't worry. Instead, put your energy into observing and gathering character traits from people in your own life so you can create dynamic and fascinating fictional characters.

Values, Beliefs, Themes

Be not afraid of life. Believe that life is worth living, and your belief will help create the fact. —*William James*

It's important to write about characters who are meaningful to you and topics about which you feel passionate, in order for your intentions and interests as a writer to come through in your work. For example, if you feel strongly about how our environment is being destroyed, you might write a story using a main character who expresses that theme. You could develop another character, most likely the antagonist, who desperately wants to turn the remaining park land into a high-priced housing development. Since the main character believes in preserving the environment, this situation not only creates conflict, but allows you to express your beliefs and values through your characters.

Putting your beliefs into a fictional story or film can be more powerful than writing an essay on the environment because your audience or readers will identify personally with your beliefs through your characters. You'll entertain your readers, while revealing your feelings about the environment.

You need to decide what is at stake for the main character and the other major characters in your story. Is it honor, pride, freedom, religion, politics? Whatever you choose as the value or belief of your characters, you must give it enough importance in the story to develop a meaningful conflict that character must overcome. The belief or the value must be specific, not abstract. If you've chosen a value such as justice, then you want to show a person receiving justice or not getting justice in your story. Other values you might want to write about are freedom, honesty, ethics, education, or loyalty.

EXERCISE
Character Beliefs and Behaviors

Make a list of all your values and beliefs, writing as quickly as you can. Where did your values and beliefs come from? School? Church? Parents? Friends? Have you ever questioned or discarded some of your values or beliefs? Are you limited by your belief system or does it enhance your relationships and your life?

Now make a list of your characters' values and belief systems. How do their values and beliefs affect their behavior in your story? Are there conflicts between the characters because of their differing belief

systems? People kill in the name of values and beliefs. Wars have been waged in the name of religion, freedom from oppression and injustice. Be certain to spend a lot of time establishing your individual characters' values and belief systems. It will help you create original characters whose values and beliefs mirror your own. ■ ■ ■

In the 1961 Pulitzer prize novel, *To Kill a Mockingbird,* by Harper Lee, lawyer Atticus Finch defends a black man in a small Southern town because he knows the man deserves a fair trial, even though the town's citizens believe he is guilty. His friends from the town become angry with Finch and even threaten him, but Finch remains committed to his client. His belief in justice is stronger than his need to be well liked and to go along with the crowd. In *To Kill a Mockingbird,* Harper Lee reveals the vast amount of prejudice and racism that existed in small Southern towns like Finch's. Through compelling characters, she is able to show how dangerous and venal racism is.

What is the purpose for writing anything if you have nothing to say as a writer? What is writing all about if it's not to share your viewpoint, your passion, or your personal vision of life, death, love, birth, relationships, and yourself? It's not necessary to state your theme in the beginning, but when you write about something that has meaning to you and is important, your message will unconsciously be made visible through the characters' actions or deliberately be revealed by a character. Writing about a topic that matters to you will give your writing a much deeper level, especially if your audience goes away intrigued with or at least provoked by your vision of the world.

Whatever value or belief you want to express, you need to put it into a story with exciting and interesting characters who are capable of carrying out the values that are the theme of the story. Theme will give your story meaning and purpose. What is your purpose for writing your particular story? What belief, value, or theme do you want to share with your audience? What is important to you and why are you writing what you're writing?

EXERCISE
Novel Intentions and Take-Away Values

As quickly as you can, write what you want your readers to feel or believe after they've read your book or short story, or have seen your film or play. How do you want to influence them? What is it you have to say that you feel passionate about and hope that they will too? You may want to do this exercise before you start creating characters for your story. It will help you find your intention for your story. It will also give your main character an internal goal to work toward, which is the theme of your story.

It is your obligation to entertain your audience, to provide them with a story peopled with characters who carry out your theme in a manner that is exciting and gives your audience enjoyment and pleasure. A story where your audience can experience a catharsis, along with your character, is a powerful story. A story that allows your characters to reach their destination transformed and changed results in a natural ending that ultimately shapes your story. ■ ■ ■

Knowing Yourself, Knowing Your Characters

He that knows himself, knows others . . . *—Charles C. Colton*

For the audience to know your characters well, you must know your characters well. Many writers create characters from the outside in rather than from the inside out because they know only enough to make the characters serve the needs of the plot and no more. This makes the characters flat and stereotypical. Your characters have to be active, not passive. They need to be proactive and struggle to overcome conflict and obstacles. They can't be acted upon, otherwise they'll be bland and incomplete.

By answering the question "Who am I?" you'll be able to form a clearer perception of yourself and your characters. It provides you with the beginning of an answer to your identity. But you also need to know who you really are so you thoroughly understand what you want to say through all of your characters.

EXERCISE

Who Are You? Who Are Your Characters?

Answer this question for yourself: "Who am I?" Take into consideration all your possible roles (wife, husband, African American, conservative, dentist, nephew, sister, teacher, poor, doctor, male, Republican, actor, mother, baseball fan, football player, dancer, reader, etc.). The roles you play form your identify and are the basis of your external self and image.

Now complete "Who am I?" using no roles. Are you able to figure out who you are without your roles? You'd be surprised how many individuals are not aware of their inner self. Make a list of who you think you are on the inside. Use adjectives you think best describe you from the inside, such as sensitive, loving, depressed, isolated, lonely, happy, etc.

After you have completed the exercises, look at the information and think how you perceive yourself. Are you more attached to your external self than you are to your internal self? By doing these exercises for yourself, you will begin to learn how you feel about yourself and who you are without roles.

Now answer "Who am I?" for your fictional characters. First complete the question "Who am I?" by listing all their roles. Next answer "Who am I?" for your characters without any roles. You will know your characters better by doing these exercises, and you'll be able to give them a definite personality and identity. Can you predict how they'll act and react in your story? What roles do your characters play in your story?

After you do the same exercise for your characters you'll have a better understanding of their identity and their internal world by seeing the real person inside each character. And you will know their self-image and how they present themselves to their world through the roles they play. ▓ ▓ ▓

Negative Inner Voices

No one can make you feel inferior without your consent.

—Eleanor Roosevelt

Most characters in stories start out with a problem, such as feeling insecure, having low self-esteem, being weak, being afraid, or being stuck in their lives. In all of our lives there is a negative voice that whispers to us and keeps us blocked and afraid to take risks. The same is true of your fictional characters. They, too, have internal negative voices that give them self-doubt, insecurities that they must overcome. At times, these voices can become very strong; at other times, they can be quieted or silenced, if only momentarily.

Try to drown out your negative voice with positive statements, even if you don't believe them. Do the same for your character. If she is afraid to go out on a date, make her talk to herself until she has the courage to accept a date. If he is afraid to call a girl for a date, let him fight his fears and call anyway.

In a wonderful teleplay that later became a movie called *Marty*, written by the outstanding writer Paddy Chayefsky, there's a poignant scene when Marty, an unattractive, shy, insecure butcher, wants to call a girl he met for a date. He practices on the phone for a long time until he gets the courage to call her. When he finally picks up the phone and calls to ask her out, she refuses. It's obvious that he hasn't had much luck in the past with women, as he is so insecure and nervous. In this touching and painful scene, the audience really identifies with the character, since we all have been rejected at one time or another in our lives. The author probably was, too.

The scene is real, the character is insecure, but good-hearted, and we all root for him. We want him to get a date and feel sad for him when he can't. This is what good character development is about: involving the reader or viewer, having them feel empathy and concern for the character.

When you can take parts of yourself and give them to your fictional characters yet make them different from you, you will have succeeded in one of the most daunting journeys you will ever take as a writer.

the psychology of characters and the writer: what makes them tick

A writer is dear and necessary for us only in the measure of
which he reveals to us the inner workings of his very soul.

—*Count Leo Tolstoy*

he psychology of the writer and the writer's frame of mind
is more important than the psychology of the characters,
because the writer *is* all the characters. Everything begins with you.
As a writing teacher and a therapist, I see the close relationship
between writers' ability to create emotionally exciting characters and
their own psychology. In fact, I would venture to say that a writer's
frame of mind is more connected to her ability to create successful
characters and stories than talent. Let me share with you what I
mean about the importance of your own psychology and frame of
mind when writing.

The Psychology of the Writer

I must write it all out, at any cost. Writing is thinking. It is
more than living, for it is being conscious of living.

—*Anne Morrow Lindbergh*

Having taught thousands of writers, I have seen some of the most
talented writers never succeed, not because of lack of ability, but because
of lack of confidence or self-worth. These gifted writers never made it
because they didn't believe in the person involved—themselves. How

you feel about yourself and your self-esteem as a person, and whether or not you have the belief in yourself to succeed, can dramatically affect the quality of your writing.

Many writers have a hard time accepting any type of rejection. They can go into a downward spiral that leads to depression and despair, even if the feedback they were given was constructive criticism. Because they have feelings of inferiority or insecurity, they take rejection as a personal attack on themselves and become blocked as writers.

On the other hand, I've consulted with average writers who've become successful because they had a belief in themselves that the talented writers didn't have. Do you see how important your sense of self-worth is when you're a writer? You want your characters to be opposites, to be contrasting and interesting, but if you only feel unsure or insecure, it's often difficult to create a psychology for your characters that is different from the way you feel inside. But you must and can do this by recognizing those characteristics or personality traits that stop you. By becoming aware of them, you can change.

Writers as Therapists

A talent for drama is not a talent for writing, but is an ability to articulate human relationships. —*Gore Vidal*

As the founder and director of the Writer's Center, I have taught character development for the past ten years. It was when I began conducting a workshop for writers who wanted to focus on how to develop psychologically layered characters with more emotional depth that I became acutely aware of what a difficult process this was for writers to learn. The contrast between my therapy clients and writers was marked: In therapy, the clients were totally immersed and emotionally involved in their character's psychology, since they were the main characters in their life stories and involved in wanting to find solutions to their problems.

By contrast, most of the writers were not emotionally involved with their characters but approached them from the outside in rather than the inside out. To get writers more emotionally connected to their characters, I began to show them how understanding their characters' psychology would give their characters the same personal passion and emotional involvement that my therapy clients had.

You can't remain distant or removed from your fictional characters. You have to become involved in their psychology so you can discover what makes them tick. Without this knowledge, you can't give any emotional depth to your fictional characters. By learning techniques for understanding the psychology of your characters, you can develop interesting and fascinating characters, thus improving your stories.

You must undertake a journey of self-discovery and self-exploration to see who you are and why you behave as you do. The reason that successful writers are able to create multifaceted and emotional characters is because they aren't afraid to explore their psyche.

What about you? Do you have the courage and the motivation to be a writer willing to explore your own psychology in order to better understand the psychology of your characters? If you want to be successful at developing characters, it's essential that you understand human nature, starting with your own.

Powerful characterization needs to come from within, and it's imperative that all writers let themselves be vulnerable, receptive, and open to taking risks in developing their characters. You must be willing to look at your own life and risk dealing with aspects of yourself that might make you uncomfortable. And you also must have the courage to be honest with yourself about how to understand your own psychology, your personality, and your authentic self and to use this knowledge to create your fictional characters.

After all, you give birth to your characters, not the other way around. The characters you put into your stories reflect your imagination and your inner structure. When you breathe life into your characters, you have to start with yourself. There are riches in most writers that are never revealed because the writers don't know how to access them or are unwilling to dig inside to bring them to the surface.

When you trigger those life forces inside you, the energy fuels your characters in a myriad of ways. Your characters become real and deep, and they allow your readers and viewers to identify with and have empathy for them.

To succeed in creating a realistic psychology for your characters and to know what makes them tick, you first have to become introspective and explore your personality. In order to understand all parts of your psychology, you'll want to study your motives, your past experiences or backstory, your patterns of behavior, and your emotions. Notice if you feel depressed, anxious, or insecure. Keep a journal to monitor your own feelings and to give you a tangible connection to your inner self.

After you start to gain more self-knowledge and discover what makes you tick, you'll be better able to create the psychology of your characters. How? By learning your character's motivation, understanding his backstory, and comprehending his behavior, you will be prepared to develop his personal psychology.

As I stated earlier, you can't give anything to your fictional characters that you can't give to yourself. That doesn't mean you can't create characters who are different from you, it just means that you need to observe yourself, understand yourself, and know yourself so that you can create characters who are contradictory, complex, and complete.

In earlier chapters, we discussed creating characters from the inside out, backstory, inner and outer motivation, and creating characters different from yourself. Now it's time to integrate all the pieces and to focus on the psychology of characters so you can write characters whose behavior is realistically motivated, and who are well-rounded human beings, with contradictions, inner struggles, and personal conflicts just like you!

The Character's Psychology

I always begin with a character or characters, and then try to think up as much action for them as possible.

—John Irving

Good writers willing to learn about their characters' psychology usually make good psychologists since they're able to comprehend the emotional depths of all their characters by studying their inner selves. In this age of psychological awareness, you must also learn how to deal with the emotional problems and the mental health issues of your characters. It's important to know how characters react to divorce, death, rape, incest, physical and emotional abuse, and post-traumatic stress.

Remember, it's the characters that people care about; the characters' psychology create their specific actions and in turn build the story. You need to become a student of the human condition. Learn to understand yourself through self-observation and to understand others by observing them at work and home, and in relationships. As you become more knowledgeable about human beings, you'll automatically be able to answer the "why" of your characters when you create them.

Characters are what stories are about, just like life is about people—who they are and what's important to them. All successful writers have a knowledge of human nature and themselves. If you want to create characters who are believable and consistent, you need to give them a realistic personality, an in-depth complexity, and a solid psychology. These elements will provide your characters with motivation, complications, and layers to peel under pressure and frustration. In other words, you need to know in advance how your characters will serve the action and what makes them transform and change.

Character Traits, Types, and Temperaments

The difference between perseverance and obstinacy is that one often comes from a strong will, and the other from a strong won't. —*Henry Ward Beecher*

Jung believed that people are either an introvert or extrovert, and that their personality reflects which one they are by the type that is dominant. The major character trait of an introvert is that she is a loner—solitary, introspective, inner-directed, and self-contained, with a dislike for crowds. On the other hand, an extrovert loves people, is good in groups, is outer-directed, popular, and confident.

If you want your character to be active, engaged with other characters and maybe even collide with them, you would portray him as an extrovert. You would use an introvert if you wanted to show a loner or a shy person. Maybe your introverted character is a mystery someone would like to discover more about. In Jane Austen's *Sense and Sensibility*, Elinor Dashwood is clearly an introvert as she observes people and reflects upon them in her quiet manner.

Many writers use Jung's character traits when creating characters who are realistic human beings. In addition to being an extrovert or introvert, Jung created four categories within each of these types. They are the thinking type, feeling type, intuitive type, and sensation type.

For example, you'd use a feeling type if you wanted to portray a warm-hearted and caring man who empathizes with those around him. Such a character could be a psychologist, social worker, nurse, or doctor.

You might use a thinking type who is more analytical and logical rather than an emotional character to portray a professor or an engineer. Putting these two types together will certainly give your characters an arena for conflict and contrasts.

The sensation type likes to operate with her five senses. This type might love the physical world of nature, or be a hedonist or Epicurean. Maybe she owns a restaurant, is a food critic, or loves music and art.

Finally, there's the intuitive type who trusts his instincts and gut feelings. He could be a leader with the courage to make decisions when others are afraid to.

Remember, your characters aren't just one type but a composite of different types. However, there is usually one type that stands out more than the others. Using these combinations can bring conflict and depth to your characters' lives.

EXERCISE

My Character Is . . .

Think of your characters as you would think of your fellow human beings. Give them the same internal problems. You need to develop the psychology of your characters to avoid the stereotypical or stock characters you see in B movies. Imagine some of the conflicts you have in your everyday life—feelings of self-doubt, insecurity, lust, hate, love, pain, loneliness, depression, and rage. Give your characters these same internal conflicts. What are your character's hopes? What does he fear? What is she struggling for? What does he desperately want? How does she feel inside herself? Is he confident? Is she insecure? Is he egotistical? Is she resentful?

Focus your character's core by creating a character trait you can describe with an adjective or adverb, e.g., "My character is selfish" or "My character is fearful." This method is an important way of helping you understand your character's psychology. As you look in a thesaurus and make a list of all the adjectives you can think of for your

character's personality, you will better understand her. But first decide what adjective best suits her overall personality.

75

After you've written down your character's most prominent personality trait, write a scene using the adjective that will describe the way he behaves. His dialogue should also portray this adjective and be consistent with his temperament. In fact, your character's personality traits and temperament will determine how other characters treat him. For example, if the adjective you've chosen for your character is "aggressive," we should see your character behave and speak in an aggressive manner. This technique will help you capture the essence of your character and find his core. ▮ ▮ ▮

EXERCISE

Understanding the Psychology of Your Characters

Think of some of your favorite films, novels, and television programs. Write some of the major characters you remember and like. Next to their names, describe what makes each character unique. Try to understand the psychology of these characters you've chosen and why you like them. Now take some of the same traits of these characters and create characters with similar qualities. Put them into a story to see if you can translate the psychology of your favorite characters into your own. ▮ ▮ ▮

Characters From the Inside

What is character but the determination of incident? What is incident but the illustration of character? —*Henry James*

Each layer of your characters can be compared with the different parts of yourself. You have a private self where all feeling, thinking, and imagination reside, and a public self, which carries your observable behavior and how you communicate with others. Many times these different selves are in conflict and can cause psychological problems.

For example, you are looking for an acting job and find the perfect part advertised in the paper. You're completely qualified for the role, but you don't go to the audition. Why? Because inside you feel insecure and unsure of your acting ability, and you're in conflict with yourself. You stay home and someone not as talented as you gets the part. Your desire to become an actor is in conflict with your lack of self-esteem.

When you develop a character from the inside out, make certain that the character's inside is different from his outside in order to develop a complicated character with internal struggles and outer calm. To achieve this, you'll first want to study the relationship between your external self and your internal self.

EXERCISE

Cause and Effect Connections

What is the relationship between your character's physical appearance and her inner world? To find the answer, ask the same question of yourself.

Look for cause-and-effect connections between all aspects of your character's life by first looking at your own. Examine connections between your character's inner life and outer world. How is your character playing a role? How is she being authentic? Does your character behave one way but feel another? Is your character congruent? How is your character incongruent?

Recall how you feel when you've gained a few pounds. If you go to a party and are sensitive about how you look, you will behave in an entirely different manner then you would if you felt you looked your best. It's amazing how you can attract people or repel them by your inner attitude and whether or not you're giving off negative or positive energy.

By creating cause-and-effect connections between your characters' physical appearances and internal perceptions, you can make them attractive to the opposite sex or repulsive. You can have them be endearing or obnoxious. By their internal personality they can be charming, while being unattractive, or exude sex appeal, while being average looking. It's the combination of their personality and their psychology that gives your characters emotional layering. ▪ ▪ ▪

Since there's no new plots under the sun, it's important for your characters to not only be good, but also outstanding. Characters can make a story stand out from all the rest. Just look at the success of the sitcom *Friends*. While hundreds of sitcoms are developed for television each year, the percentage of those that are dropped is relatively very high. *Friends* has succeeded year after year because its characters are universal, compelling, and layered.

Another example of a character who has staying power is James Bond, created by British novelist Ian Fleming. For the past forty years, Bond has remained an exciting character who's popular with both readers and viewers because of his originality, magnetic charm, and fearlessness. He is a ladies' man, a bon vivant, and a courageous hero.

Successful characters display many other personality traits besides their major one. They're complex because they have depth that continues to be revealed throughout the story, rather than being stereotypical characters who don't have staying power. By creating contrasting inner and outer selves, you'll create multifaceted characters with many personality traits, and who contrast and collide with one another.

Successful writers consider their characters' internal feelings, going deeply into their past, asking pertinent questions along the way.

EXERCISE
Layering Your Character's Psychological Profile
Return to the psychological profile you started for your character in chapter two, and think about the following questions.

Who raised your character? Did he have a happy childhood? Where did he grow up? Were his parents divorced or were they happily married? Did he have any brothers or sisters, or was he the only child? Was he the oldest child or the youngest? In school did he have a lot of friends? Was he a loner? Was he popular? Was he an athlete? Was he the class clown? Did he always have a different date? Was he a good student, or did he cut class? How did he relate to his parents, siblings, friends, relatives?

One successful sitcom writer who consulted with me said that after she'd learned how to use her own psychology for her characters, she set the pace in the writers' meetings. She told me that the meeting sounded like therapy sessions because as each writer shared his or her personal life experiences, they all began to sound like budding psychologists, and they started to develop backstories for their characters by using their own pasts.

By the time you finish creating a psychological profile for each character you will determine the traumas, crisis, or experiences from childhood that have influenced his psychology. Is he depressed, anxious, or nervous? Does he have low self-esteem or is he confident? Is he an extrovert or an introvert? Is he intuitive or feeling? Is he a sensationalist or a thinking type?

By creating a psychological profile, you will know your character's parents, grandparents and even great-grandparents. By understanding the psychology of your characters, you'll be able to understand their behavior and develop the necessary motivation for it, so you don't lose the interest of your readers or viewers. ■ ■ ■

A Search for Reasons

It's never too late—in fiction or in life—to revise.
—*Nancy Thayer*

As a writer behaving like a psychologist, you are always probing more deeply inside your character's skin, continually questioning his behavior. You are searching for reasons for his actions and creat- ing motivation for them. By asking probing questions, you'll develop characters who are layered and who will reveal themselves under pressure. This gives your characters action and your story momentum. Never stop questioning your characters and how they became the people they are.

To give you an example of how you have to take your character's psychology into account when you create her behavior, let's look at the following illustration. Suppose your character has just moved to Los Angeles and is looking for a place to live. As we discovered in chapter three, wanting shelter is a basic need. If your character has the time and the money, she'll have a lot of choices. She can choose a realtor to look for a home until she finds the right one. She can choose where she wants to live—maybe in a posh area of Beverly Hills or Santa Monica. So she gives the realtor her preference for location and the style of home she wants. The only problem she might encounter is finding a house she likes.

But what if your character is limited by a strict budget and still wants to live in those areas? What does she do? Her motivation is strong, but her bank account isn't. She might have to look for a long time until she finds the right home for the right price, maybe one that's in foreclosure. Or she might settle for a lesser home in the right area. Still, if she is desperate to find something immediately and can't find anything affordable, she might not to be able to buy a home and may have to rent an apartment instead. But what if she can't afford anything in the location she desires? Then she needs to look in another area and compromise not only on location, but also on the size of the apartment. Now our character has made many compromises. Depending on her psychology, she could be accepting, frustrated, angry, or feeling sorry for herself. But what if she doesn't have any luck finding anything in her price range? What if she only has one day to find a place and still hasn't found one? What will she do?

You must consider not only a character's motivation (needing shelter), you must also consider her internal makeup. If she is a social climber, she might settle for a single apartment in order to live in an upwardly mobile location to maintain her image. If she's desperate, she might borrow money from her parents. But let's say she loses her job and doesn't have enough money for the first and last months' rent. What will she do? If she doesn't have a family who can lend her money and if she has no friends, she won't be able to rent an apartment at all.

Now her situation is even more desperate. If she is industrious or imaginative, she may offer to manage an apartment building in exchange for free rent. Or she might sell her computer or CD player to get the rent money. But if she can't raise money, she might cope by drinking or taking drugs. Even worse, if she has no morals, she might break into a home to steal money for the rent or mug someone. If she's extremely beautiful and a sociopath, she might pretend she's in love with an older, wealthy man so she can live off his money. If she feels hopeless she might head into a downward spiral and end up sleeping on the streets, homeless.

This illustration shows you how a character's psychology determines her choices and actions. You can see how her values and beliefs, past experiences, self-image, morality, personality, and abilities will also influence her psychological makeup. Her personal choices will be influenced by her self-image and her abilities to reach her goal—her need for shelter.

Yet, it is the degree of her desperation and motivation that will determine what lengths she'll go to obtain shelter. Don't ever say, "My character would never steal," or "My character would never cheat." Given enough desperation and faced with a harsh environment, your character can be motivated to steal, lie, cheat, or even die for something she wants and needs.

EXERCISE

Growing, Coping, and Internalizing

How does your character deal with her childhood memories? What type of neuroses does your character have? What idio-syncrasies does she manifest? What is her relationship with her boss? Her parents? Her friends? Her lovers? What secrets does she have? What fears does she hide? What makes her anxious? What makes her insecure? What traumas from her past still haunt her? What childhood abuse affects her in her present? What negative messages does she constantly hear? Is she confident on the outside and insecure on the inside? What is her public persona? Is she congruent? Is she beautiful, but on the inside does she believe she's ugly? Is she difficult to relate to? What things does she obsess about? Is she afraid of making a commitment?

As you find answers to all of the above questions, you are furthering your search for reasons for your character's actions, emotions, and motivations. Through this process, you will build fresh, deep, and unique characters every time you write a story, novel, play, or script. ■ ■ ■

Characters and Internal Struggles

What wound did ever heal but by degrees?
—*William Shakespeare*

In every story you write you need to determine your character's bottom line. Human beings are capable of doing almost anything under the right circumstances, especially in life and death situations.

The way your character satisfies her needs depends on what choices are available to her at a given time. What if she is hungry and happens to be in prison or in rehab for addictions? In each case she is at the mercy of other people, and her behavior is restricted by her superiors and regulations. She's unable to make the choices she needs to make because there would be harmful consequences to her actions if she didn't have permission.

Remember not only to deal with your character's needs, but also with how he tries to meet his needs. This depends on the desperation of the need, the environment, his psychology, his attitudes, and his perception. The most important determination for behavior will be the many characteristics and traits that make up his personality and psychology.

How your characters act or react will be determined by the psychological makeup you have created for them. Your audience will understand and believe in your character as he reveals himself under pressure, only if you have done a good job in making whatever he does believable and consistent with his personality and psychology. Your readers and viewers will root for your characters and sympathize with their plight, even in cases where they don't succeed, as long as your characters struggle for what they need.

When dealing with obstacles your characters need to overcome, the struggle is of prime importance. Give your characters the psychology they need to continue the fight. You also need to continue in the face of obstacles to get the audience to root for your characters' success.

EXERCISE

For Every Action . . .

What issues or situations are important enough to you to make you fight or go the distance? Are you adamant about religion, politics, principles, values, or beliefs? What extremes would you go to in order to defend your position? Answer these questions for yourself: "What would I fight for?" "What would I die for?" Write about it.

Now answer the same questions for your characters. What would they fight for? What would they die for? Write a scene showing a character in your story being passionate about an ideal, idea, or principle, and fighting for it. Now write about a character in your story who is willing to die for a belief or cause.

83

By recognizing those values, beliefs, and principles that are important and sacred to you, you'll be able to give your characters beliefs, principles, and values for which they will fight. Keep focused on your goal of being a successful writer who is able to understand the psychology of your characters and most importantly, the psychology of yourself. ■ ■ ■

creating your villain: tapping the shadow

> Everyone carries a shadow, and the less it is embodied in the
> individual's conscious life, the blacker and denser it is.
>
> —C.G. Jung

*I*n order to create exciting and unique villains you first have
to study why some villains in fiction and films have been so
successful, while others are stereotypical and clichéd. There are villains
portrayed in books and films who are not criminals including rogues,
manipulators, liars, femme fatales, overbearing bosses, heartbreakers,
and heartless step-parents. However, in this chapter I'll be focusing
on the extreme type of villains who exhibit murderous tendencies and
traits because writers often turn these types of villains into caricatures.

Creating multifaceted villains is one of the biggest challenges writers confront and devoting a chapter to real villains will help you learn
what elements it takes to develop an original villain, one who is both
frightening and fascinating. You need to become familiar with the
different psychological types who inevitably become villains and criminals. Learning how a criminal thinks will allow you to convincingly
write about one. Before you are able to create lifelike villains, you
should become aware of their specific character traits, especially those
indigenous to psychopaths, sociopaths, serial killers, serial rapists, pedophiles, and psychotics in order to have your villains be memorable
and menacing. It's important not only to write a good story, but to
develop believable villains based in truth.

According to Carl Jung, each of us has a shadow archetype that resides in our collective unconscious. The shadow archetype is the dark side where all of your desires and aggressions hide; it's the side you may try to disown because you don't want to admit you have such feelings as rage, envy, lust, greed, and jealousy. But whether or not you recognize these feelings, they're inside you. They are lying in wait for the right time and the right place to emerge.

Tapping Your Shadow

If you gaze long into an abyss, the abyss will gaze back into you. —*Friedrich Wilhelm Nietzsche*

The shadow, which has become lost to your conscious mind through repression, needs to be acknowledged and owned before you can put the dark side into your villains. But first you need to understand why you originally disowned your shadow.

As discussed in the last chapter, we have many different selves and archetypes in our collective unconscious. Often, our shadow archetype is at war with other parts of ourselves. We repress our shadow selves in order to please other people, and to repress our bad experiences or shameful thoughts. We don't want to admit to our darker feelings because they make us uncomfortable. As young children we're told not to have bad feelings, so we push them underground in an effort to banish them from our psyche when our parents, teachers, or others disapprove.

We all need to be acculturated so that we can adapt and be stable members of society. We learn how to function in a world with rules, laws, and consequences. By trying to be accepted and liked, we soon find ways to conceal our dark and primitive feelings, burying them beneath the false face we wear for the public. The person who adjusts to society is one who has acceptable characteristics on the outside. It's true that we must be in balance, and this often requires a great deal of work. To balance parts of yourself is to be aware of your dark feelings. The villain or serial killer is out of balance, and his dark side has overtaken him.

What better way to try to meet your shadow than through creating villains. As you become acquainted with your own dark side and get to know it through some of the exercises you'll do in this chapter, you will reclaim that part of you who is capable of creating multi-dimensional villains. As you release your own anger, jealousy, greed, resentments, lust, and rage, and put those negative feelings into your villains, you'll discover the secret of creating layered villains with universal appeal—villains with smiling faces masking sick fantasies.

There is a price to pay when you ignore these feelings. When you deny they exist, they burrow deeper inside you. When the shadow is repressed, we can become depressed, and suffer ailments including ulcers, headaches, and chronic tiredness—all because we're not expressing our anger, rage, and other dark emotions.

People love thrillers such as *The Poet* by Michael Connelly, *Carrie* by Stephen King, or *Kiss the Girls* by James Patterson. These suspense thrillers help readers release their own pent-up tension and fears. When the villain is caught and the hero saves the day, readers are able to experience a catharsis that acts as an emotional release of feelings they don't openly express, such as sexual tension, rage, lust, terror, greed, and revenge.

As a creator of villains, you want to become a partner with your dark side and learn to create such releases for your dark side and those of your readers. You do this by becoming aware of darker feelings of which you are often ashamed. Accept them as part of your being, rather than pushing them down inside. It's okay to have dark feelings; in fact it's part of being human. Embrace your darker feelings and infuse your villainous characters with them to create characters who are adept at expressing their darker feelings without shame or guilt.

There is also a positive side of the shadow—it's a powerful source of creativity and imagination. But first, you need the courage to embrace your shadow and its creative energy in order to build exciting fictional villains who are realistic and frightening. Method writing, which was described earlier, is a powerful creative technique to use for creating villains. How? By remembering an experience from your past and using your five senses, you can recall your feelings. By recalling details through your sensory writing, you will then be able to better portray villains and their sensual selves. First you need to do what actors do and recall your sensory memory by tapping into your dark side, as well as into your own specific memories from the past.

EXERCISE
Feelings of Fear

Using your sensory memory, recall a time when you were very frightened by a particular person or situation. Visualize the scene and recapture the feelings of fear that you had at the time. Be in the scene with all of your senses. Using first person, write about it as fast as you can without lifting your pen from the paper. Write for at least fifteen minutes, and paint a dark picture with your words. Put your feeling into your characters, and write about the person or situation that scared you.

After you've finished writing the scene read it without editing. Were you scared when you wrote it? When you read it? Are you surprised that this particular person or situation came up? What was it about this person or situation that scared you?

Now see if you can take these feelings of being frightened and translate them into your protagonist or victim. Put the frightening qualities of the other person into your villain. By putting your honest fears into your characters, you'll be able to portray realistic and frightening villains.

As a writer who wants to create original villains, you have the opportunity to use your shadow. Make it your partner. Let all your darker feelings emerge into your fictional villains so they'll frighten your audience. Writing about villains provides you with a creative outlet by giving you the opportunity to express all of your unacceptable feelings on the page. ■ ■ ■

Tapping the Universal Shadow

The mind is its own place, and in itself can make a Heaven of
Hell, a Hell of Heaven. —*John Milton*

Beside your own personal shadow, there is also a collective shadow consciousness in the world. When you create villains, you want to put them into a unique setting or world, but you also want to be aware of what's going on in the world in which you're living so that you can portray a villain who modern readers will respond to.

At times, it can seem as though there is a collective shadow spinning out of control. Violence has become an integral part of our culture more than ever before. The collective shadow seems to have exploded, and, as a writer, it is imperative you become aware of what is happening in the world. If you write about villains who are living now, you'll need to create true-to-life villains whose motives will be more complex than ever before.

Perhaps your villain is motivated to kill more out of political or religious beliefs rather than just psychological aberrations. Or perhaps you want to create a political villain but also show that her zealousness and fanaticism are based on distorted thinking or a warped belief system.

EXERCISE

Writing the Darker Side of Life

Recall a villain from the news or current events. What qualities does that villain have that you could use for your villain?

How is his dark side portrayed? What motivates him? Create a villain who is modeled after a contemporary villain. Ask the same questions **for your own character. What motivates her? Religion? Politics? Values? How does your villain manifest her dark side? If your villain has a dark side based on a warped belief system, describe it in detail.**

The more you get beneath your villain's veneer, the more complex your villain will become. Try to create a new type of villain who is related to what is happening in your world. Practice the above exercise for different areas and discover how to write exciting villains who are diversified and dark. ■ ■ ■

Tapping Your Villain's Shadow

Humanity is an ocean; if a few drops of the ocean are dirty, the ocean does not become dirty. —*Mahatma Gandhi*

As we discussed in chapter three, motivation is one of the basic components in building believable characters. However, it's often difficult to motivate psychopaths and sociopaths because they don't respond to normal behaviors, thoughts, or feelings. To have your villains ring true to readers, you need to know what makes them tick.

Your villains will be caricatures if you make them all black and white. Exciting villains must be filled with shades of gray. You'll have to give your villains a complete backstory, so you can discover how they became criminals. You also must give them complex inner motives such as history of being abused, deprived of parental guidance or love, or having emotional problems in early relationships. These circumstances will give you the necessary motivation to create villains who are believable and real.

This inner motivation you give your villains will help make their irrational and criminal behaviors seem believable, even if it's difficult for you and other normal people to comprehend their behavior. As you read this chapter, you'll become familiar with the criminal mind and the different types of criminal behavior.

Faye Kellerman, a prolific mystery novelist, said that rather than being called "whodunits," suspense novels should be called "whydunits," since the writer needs to find answers for the villain's psychology to give reasons for his unreasonable behavior by constantly asking "Why?"

To write realistic villains you first must ask and then answer the question, "Why?"

EXERCISE

Understanding Your Villain's Motivation

Answer in detail why your villain became who he is today. What was it in his childhood or in his makeup that made him into a villain? What type of villain have you created? An obvious one? A sinister one? Have you created a villain who is charming and disarming, but sick and vicious inside? Is your villain motivated? Is the motivation believable? Describe your villain in detail. ▪ ▪ ▪

Profiling Your Villain

> In this world everything changes except good deeds and bad deeds; these follow you as the shadow follows the body.
>
> —*Anonymous*

Obviously, you have to understand the makings of a criminal or at least get a grasp on some of her most dominant traits if you want to create your own fictional villains. Although there are always exceptions to any rule, the following psychological profile was developed by forensic psychiatrists and FBI profilers and is used to identify specific traits that are indigenous for serial killers and psychopaths.

Profiles for Psychopaths and Serial Killers

In psychological terms, psychopathic traits are listed under Antisocial Personality Disorder (which we'll discuss in greater detail in chapter ten). Under the general heading of psychopath, there are a variety of characteristics, and as you become familiar with them, you'll be better prepared to instill these traits into your fictional characters to give your villains layers and depth.

It's important for you to base your villains on some of the real traits and characteristics that have been identified by crime fighting departments. It's also helpful to do research and to become familiar with the wealth of material on the criminal mind and crime. Then, you can use your creativity and imagination to expand and embellish your villains so they become original.

Criminal profilers list the following traits for psychopaths who can become serial killers: male, white, isolated, in their twenties or thirties, no empathy, vivid imaginations, act out fantasies, callous, restless, grandiose, resentful, inability to love, impulsive, remorseless, aggressive, no conscience, sadistic, inability for intimacy, insecure, and proficient liars.

Most serial killers are preoccupied with the need for thrills and excitement. They are often fueled by a strong fantasy life, which eventually drives them to murder. In some cases, beating, torturing, and manipulating their victims even sexually excites them, especially when they can wield power and control over their victims, most of whom are women and children.

Writers have used some infamous real-life serial killers as prototypes for fictional creations. In the book *Psycho*, by Robert Bloch, the villain, Norman Bates, was based on a real serial killer named Ed Gein. Gein was completely tied to his mother, even after she'd died. He used women's body parts to decorate his home. Gein liked to rob women's graves, carve off bits of their body and make costumes out of them that he would then wear. He made lamps out of female skin and organs. He was so deranged that he thought he was a part of his mother when he dressed up in the female skins.

92   In *Psycho,* Norman Bates has a cruel mother, much like Ed Gein had. Mrs. Bates is, at times, kind to Norman, but she also abuses him physically and emotionally. The horrendous background he suffers is responsible for his later psychotic behavior.

When he's grown, and danger or desire threatens him, Norman splits off from himself and disassociates from being Norman Bates. He dresses up like his dead mother and "becomes" her when he kills. He is able to murder people as his mother because he believes that nothing can harm him when he is her. His personality split is so absolute that he puts his shadow into his mother. By the end of the book, he has lost Norman Bates forever. Like Ed Gein, the fictional Norman Bates spends the rest of his life in a mental institution.

EXERCISE
Serial Killers and Inner Conflicts

After you study and become familiar with the serial killer traits in the above profile, apply some or all of them to create your villain for your story. Which real-life villains frighten you? What is it about him or her that scares you? Using the same traits that scare you, create your villain and give her realism by integrating these very traits into her character. Use your imagination to make her fresh, complex, and frightening. Develop inner conflicts for her childhood that still affect her.

Now put your character into a scene in which her dark side is revealed. This process will make your villains more sinister, evil, and exciting. ■ ■ ■

Profiles for Sociopaths

A sociopath is a person who has a lack of conscience and cares only about fulfilling her own needs, even if it's at the expense of other people. Even though these traits are similar to the psychopath, the sociopath usually isn't a killer. However, they also violate other people without feeling guilt or empathy. A good example of a fictional socio- **93** path is the character of Fagin in Charles Dickens' *Oliver Twist.* Fagin has a gang of young boys who he trains to pick pocket, rob, steal, lie, and cheat for him, yet he doesn't do these things himself.

Sociopaths appear sincere and can make people believe them when they're lying. They are great scam and con artists, and have the ability to impress and exploit others and their weaknesses, without guilt or remorse. They can easily make friends but are unable to maintain good relationships because they're unable to be honest with others and themselves.

Sociopaths have a marked inability to love or be loved because they are so egocentric, and they're unable to bond with the opposite sex. Although not all sociopaths are necessarily criminals, many have aggressive behaviors that they act out through their anger. They can pass as normal, but are extremely adept at being insincere and manipulative to others.

Their behavior is often caused by some type of family dysfunction in childhood, such as lack of parental control or guidance. For example, they may come from broken homes or have an absentee parent. As teens they can be extremely aggressive, and often tyrannize or bully others. They may join gangs with members like themselves, and as teenagers, they're frequently runaways. They never feel accountable for their behavior and are always blaming others; unfortunately, many get away with such behavior.

Nurture or Nature

I found one day in school a boy of medium size ill-treating a smaller boy. I expostulated, but he replied: "The bigs hit me, so I hit the babies; that's fair." In these words he epitomized the history of the human race. —*Bertrand Russell*

Do you believe there are children who are just "bad seeds" from birth? Or could their brain chemistry be off? Could they lack some type of emotional capability to feel empathy for others? Or is every criminal really a victim of his childhood or environment? Are criminals simply victims of being born to the wrong parents?

These questions have no concrete answers and have caused endless debate. Some feel that a criminal is formed because of his environment and parental influences, while others believe genetics and heritage are the culprits. Whichever road you take when you're creating your villains, whether it be nurture or nature, you must base it in reality.

The Bad Seed, a novel by William March, brings this debate into the world of fiction. The main character, an eight-year old girl named Rhonda Penmark, is pretty, precocious, and perfect except for the fact that she's an evil murderer, even though she's a youngster.

The motivation March gives Rhonda for being homicidal is that her maternal grandmother also was a murderer, even killing all of her children except Rhonda's mother, who escaped.

This book provides just one view on whether a person can be born with a propensity toward evil. It's up to you to decide whether you will create a villain based on the premise that he is a natural born killer or that he's evil because of an abusive childhood and trauma. To create unique and unusual villains you will either make them victims of nature or of nurture, with them being victims of genetics or of a traumatic childhood.

There is evidence that due to brain chemistry, genetics, and heritage some individuals have aberrant behaviors and lead lives of crime, in spite of being the products of loving parents and having a good childhood. If you want to base your villain on being a victim of nature, there are some serious inappropriate behaviors that certain children exhibit in childhood. Many of them act out by bullying, torturing and killing animals, setting fires, showing lack of guilt, and engaging in rebellion, chronic lying, aggression, bed-wetting, and defiance.

If you make your character villainous because of her childhood, then perhaps it's because she didn't receive the necessary love or nurturing during childhood. This lack could be the basis of her sociopathic or psychopathic behavior. Perhaps your villain comes from a broken home, or a family where one of the parents is abusive. Even though most people who come from broken homes don't become sociopathic or psychopathic, divorced parents and broken homes can be a contributing factor. You can also make your villainous character come from a home where the parents are addicts or alcoholics, which also can be another important factor in developing sociopathic and psychopathic personalities.

Children who are abused become filled with rage. Since abused children can't retaliate against their parents, they take out their hidden rage by picking on those who are more vulnerable than they are— like younger children or small animals. Their behavior can escalate from bullying to beatings to torture to maiming.

If your villain is evil due to her environment, consider some of the possible contributors: abusive parents, seductive mothers, overly strict fathers, alcoholic or drug addicted parents, incest, beatings, torture, or trauma. You need to search for reasons for your villain's behavior in the present by finding the answers in her past history. That's why you should know so much more of her past than you reveal in your story. Whatever reasons you choose for your villain's behavior, remember that in real life, as well as fiction, many criminals refer to childhood traumas as the cause of their life of crime and chaos. In court their defense lawyers may try to bring up their client's upbringing to the jury, in an attempt to show the cause of how they came to lead a life of crime and that their client wasn't evil as a child, but a victim of an unhappy and traumatic childhood. Almost every prisoner blames someone other than herself for her crime. There always seems to be "if it weren't for. . . ." The abuse excuse has become very popular among criminals and their lawyers in their defense.

EXERCISE
Unleashing Pent-Up Aggression
Fill in the blanks for your own fictional villains, "If it weren't for . . ." and write the backstory of their childhood and how they became the way the are now.

Does that help you get a better profile of your villain? It should give you helpful information of why he thinks of himself as a victim of his past, thereby justifying his present criminal behavior. ■ ■ ■

Just like a normal human being, a villain is capable of loving and hating the same person, and of having opposing feelings and committing acts of good and evil. These opposing drives create conflict and frustration within villainous characters, too. Such conflicts should be the basis of the obstacles put in your villain's path to thwart his evil plans or to prevent him from killing his next victim.

In Mario Puzo's *The Godfather*, Michael Corleone, the youngest son of the Godfather, is resistant to becoming part of the Mafia and plans to stay out of the family business and lead a normal life. When his father is almost killed, the drive to protect his family and to avenge the attempt on his father's life set him on a different and murderous path. This radical change in direction alters his personality and ultimately allows his shadow persona to become an all-consuming force.

Latent Villainous Tendencies

The torment of human frustration, whatever its immediate cause, is the knowledge that the self is in prison, its vital force and "mangled mind" leaking away in lovely, wasteful self-conflict. —*Elizabeth Drew*

Whether or not you're aware of your shadow, it is always there. Many people try to ignore their shadow self through addictions such as alcohol, drugs, or food. But these outlets don't work, and the shadow's presence remains with you.

We must accept all parts of ourselves: the good and evil, the dark and light, the highs and lows. That's the secret to becoming a writer capable of creating multidimensional villains. No matter how we appear on the outside, the shadow is smoldering inside, working non-stop, lurking on the sidelines, waiting to get us. We often project our darker feelings onto other people when we disown the parts of ourselves that we hate to admit we have.

It's important for you to become aware of those people who have qualities you dislike and of whom you are critical. More often than not, you'll discover that they are manifesting qualities that you deny in yourself. You may want to put this dynamic into place with your hero and villain, too.

By using projection and denial in your characters you will be giving them emotional layers and depth. Maybe your hero hates a quality in the villain that's exactly the same trait he dislikes and finds unacceptable in himself. For example, in the novel *Elmer Gantry*, by Sinclair Lewis, Gantry portrays himself to the public as a moralistic preacher and lectures his congregation about the evils of sin, while, in fact, he is sinning all the time in his personal life.

Remember that many villains in books and films aren't serial killers or psychopaths. They are just like you and me, but beneath their smile is a sinister personality or sociopathic traits.

The Disowned Shadow Gone Awry

"One soweth and another reapeth" is a verity that applies to evil as well as good. —*George Eliot*

Psychopaths, sociopaths, and other criminal types allow their shadow to be the dominant part of their personality. Their dark side takes control, and, even if they wanted to, these criminals couldn't stop themselves.

The disowned shadow is the dark side in your self that you unconsciously try to ignore. We try to control it, but can we really? It's not just the obvious hard-core criminals who are out of control, sometimes there are ordinary people whose shadow has taken over. Rich or poor, CEO of a conglomerate or janitor, father or son, mother or daughter, the shadow can begin to dominate a person, who, up until then, has tried to hold his impulses in check.

Here are a few literary examples where a seemingly stable character is overtaken by his or her shadow and yet isn't necessarily a criminal:

1. A mother who is overcome with grief at the loss of her young daughter cheats on her husband with a detective working her daughter's case. (*The Lovely Bones*, by Alice Sebold)

2. A previously quiet, law-abiding man joins an underground revolutionary organization that's bent on bringing down the government—and he does it all for a forbidden love affair. (*1984*, by George Orwell)

In fiction and in life, individuals are capable of becoming villains under the right circumstances. In fact, you can deliberately motivate your fictional characters to go down into their inner depths and become capable of committing murder or mayhem. You can create multidimensional villains who are in positions of power, prestige, and popularity or who are average in every way possible.

EXERCISE

Letting the Shadow Take Over

Set up certain circumstances where the dark side of your character takes over. How does the story begin, and why does the villain commit a crime? Remember to use your five senses and really get in touch with your own dark side.

Sometimes the dark side emerges when the right circumstances take over. When there is a crisis such as a death, divorce, financial

ruin, or undue stress, and individuals feel out of control, the dark side can overtake their personalities and motivate them to desperate measures. Of course, there are other shadow stimuli that motivate criminal acts such as greed, lust, revenge, jealousy, and rage.

The shadow is always with each of your characters. The difference between a villain and a hero can be a very fine line, and a person becomes a villain when the shadow self becomes the dominant self and takes over. ■ ■ ■

Shadow Behavior Reflected in Expressions

An enemy generally says and believes what he wishes.
—*Thomas Jefferson*

There are some phrases that are connected to the shadow feelings of being out of control, of losing it, and then feeling shame and regret afterward. For the average person, this occasionally happens and, hopefully, isn't often repeated. On the other hand, villains often might have these outbursts and not apologize for them unless they're in a vulnerable situation. Then they might use an expression such as "I don't know what came over me," "I lost my head," or "The devil made me do it," in order to avoid taking personal responsibility.

Such expressions have to do with repressed feelings that just exploded and were beyond the individual's control to stop them. Of course, your villains might never use these expressions, because their shadow is their dominant trait and they would be acting out their fantasies rather than apologizing for them.

EXERCISE
Expressing Anger and Frustration

Make a list of all the expressions you might say when you lose your temper. How do you behave when you're angry or frustrated? Do you drive too fast or throw a temper tantrum? What does it feel like to lose control? How do you feel after your outburst? Do you suffer from feelings of shame and guilt because you've "lost it"? After you've made your personal list, write a scene using your villain to show the release of anger, rage, or resentment through inappropriate behavior. Your villain probably wouldn't feel guilty; however a cunning villain could easily say "I don't remember a thing" to cover his real motives and his dark side. ■ ■ ■

EXERCISE
Shadow Manifestations

Can you recall anyone from your life who appeared nice on the surface, but was an extreme control freak underneath? What did he do? How did he manifest his coldness and need for power? Write a scene about this person, a villain who is not obvious—someone who can pass as normal, but will stop at nothing to get his way. Use your imagination and combine reality with fiction. Remember that a villain doesn't need to be a literal killer, but can kill figuratively. ■ ■ ■

Making Your Villain Popular

The good end happily, the bad unhappily. That is what fiction means. —*Oscar Wilde*

Earlier in this chapter, I discussed the characteristics of serial killers and psychopaths. You can read them over and choose the ones you feel fit the type of villain you need in your story. You also can read about actual cases of actual serial killers and base your villains on these terrifying real-life killers.

Thomas Harris, the creator of the memorable villain Dr. Hannibal Lecter, is said to have based his character on several real-life psychopaths. What is important is that he did his research and knew what characteristics made up the criminal mind of the psychopathic serial killer.

Hannibal Lecter is the villain in three suspense thrillers: *Red Dragon, The Silence of the Lambs,* and *Hannibal.* A brilliant former psychiatrist, he has become a serial killer because of a horrific incident involving himself and his younger sister. Not only does he kill people, but he cannibalizes his victims as well.

Lecter is fascinating, unpredictable, and unique. He is the epitome of evil and yet endearing in an odd way. He's cunning and cold, charming and disarming, worldly and weird. He's a bon vivant, with Epicurean tastes in food and drink, but also a fondness for human body parts. At one minute he can be a masterful psychiatrist, playing with the mind of FBI agent Clarice Starling, and the next minute he is muzzled and shackled to prevent him from violently attacking his guards. What a complex villain!

Hannibal Lecter is so universally popular, he's almost become an archetypal villain like Dracula or Mr. Hyde. In fact, he is one of the most well-known modern villains. All three novels have been turned into highly successful films. Lecter is the type of villain you should strive to create in your stories. Build villains who are filled with dichotomies: charming and cold, worldly and wicked, and educated and evil.

On HBO's Emmy award-winning series *The Sopranos,* the main character, Tony Soprano, is a Mafia chieftain, with a real family and a Mafia one. His character is a murderer, and yet he's frequently portrayed sympathetically as a concerned father, husband, brother, and son. Even though he's frequently seen committing coldhearted murders, he also suffers from anxiety attacks and sees a psychiatrist for therapy and for anti-depressants. Like Lecter, Tony Soprano is a multifaceted character. Aside from being villainous, he is a real person, one who worries about his disintegrating marriage and his children. He is a contrast in complicated feelings—a family man and a murdering man, a caring father and a cunning killer.

If you want to create exciting villains who are popular, let your readers be fascinated, intrigued, and horrified by them all at the same time. By understanding the dark sides of Hannibal Lector and Tony Soprano, you'll be able to build layers of opposing drives and needs into your own villains.

EXERCISE
Adding Complexities to Your Villain

Create a villain who is a contradiction, complex and filled with inconsistencies. Color your villain in shades of gray, not just in black or white. Give him some qualities that are redeeming, even in the face of his evil deeds. Now put this villian in a story where he is faced with an opponent who wants to prevent him from getting what he wants. What does your villain do? How does he change when his goal is being thwarted?

Great villains are just like other people in that they're filled with polarities. They can't be all bad, just as heroes can't be all good. Employ your own shadow, and put all your darker feelings into portraying realistic villains who operate from their dark side and yet are able to fool people by showing their charm to outsiders. ■ ■ ■

EXERCISE
Understanding and Acknowledging Your Shadow

List some of your personal traits that reflect your dark side. How do you hide your shadow self? How do you reveal your dark side? Put some of these behaviors into your villain. How does your villain express her dark side? How does your villain hide her shadow? List your villain's buried character traits that reflect her dark side. Use these hidden character traits to create a multidimensional villain.

By now you've learned how to access your shadow self. Hopefully, you will be able to put all of your liberated feelings into your villains. Building villains is an "inside job," and starts with you accepting the self you once repressed. You will find that when you accept rather than disown your shadow, you'll create villains who are complicated and alive.

Writing allows you the opportunity to express all of your unacceptable feelings in your villains. By letting your own dark side, fears, and fantasies onto the page, you'll create realistic, original, and unique villains who aren't all bad and heroes who aren't all good. And your villains will be incredibly credible and withstand the test of time. ■ ■ ■

the heart of drama: injecting feelings into your characters

Good writing is supposed to evoke sensation in the reader—
not the fact that it is raining, but the feel of being rained
upon. —*E.L. Doctorow*

*I*n this chapter you'll discover the importance of embracing your own emotions. If you can reconnect with your emotions—rage, joy, love, hate, anger, lust, sorrow—you'll be better able to inject them into your characters. Without emotions your characters will be empty shells, and your stories will be superficial. Emotions will enable you to write rich, layered characters.

The word emotion derives from the Latin word *emovere*, which means to excite, to move, to stir, or to agitate. Emotional states are relatively short levels of arousal and desires to act. Some emotions, such as fear, joy, disgust, pity, and love, are regarded as relatively momentary feelings, which can motivate action and activity, and then subside. Other emotions are intensely experienced states, like rage, anger, terror, grief, and fear, in which an individual's behavior may be erratic or irrational.

Emotions should be the lifeblood of your characters and stories. Without emotional characters you are writing about events, but you're not drawing in your audience. You should create emotional characters so your reader will become so emotionally involved with them, he'll forget he's reading a book, seeing a play, or viewing a film. If you can provide your characters with emotional conflicts, readers can be completely engrossed in the emotional world of your story.

The emotions of characters such as Emma Bovary in Gustave Flau-
bert's *Madam Bovary* and Scarlett O'Hara in Margaret Mitchell's
Gone with the Wind allow readers to identify with them and root for
them, even though they both have flaws. The greatest characters touch
the feelings of the audience in different cultures and societies, with-
standing the test of time. Such characters allow the audience to experience empathy for them because the characters have an emotional
depth that resonates with readers and viewers.

Your Character's Emotional and Psychological World

Only connect the prose and the passion, and both will be ex-
alted, and human love will be seen at its highest.

—*E.M. Forster*

As a modern writer you must show a deep understanding of the
emotional and psychological world of your characters if you want
your characters to be taken seriously. Your awareness of these worlds
enables your readers to become sensitive to the unseen motivations
of your characters and the multiple layers of their personalities. As I
discussed earlier, when creating characters, you always have to start
with yourself because the characters you put into your stories are all
part of you.

By going behind the facade of your characters, you'll write ones
with real meaning and purpose. Feelings once submerged, will enrich
your writing life and give your characters an emotional reality. When
writing emotion-filled characters, you'll need to answer questions
about their emotional lives, such as: Is your character depressed? How
does your main character emotionally relate to other characters? What
is the emotional makeup of your main character and your other major
characters?

After you read this chapter, you'll better understand the importance of knowing how to inject emotions into your characters, and you'll be able to answer these questions for all of your characters in any story you write.

Emotions are energy, and when you write emotional characters, you are giving them energy and momentum to take action and to overcome obstacles, especially emotional ones. Writing personal stories gives you the opportunity to create characters with strong feelings and layers of emotional depth because such stories come from deep emotional truths. You create characters who will involve and represent your passions, loves, hates, joys, sorrows, resentments, and fears.

Many of you might say, "Well, that's obvious, every good writer knows you need emotions in your characters and stories." However, you'd be surprised how many writers have no idea how to give their characters emotions or how to release their own emotions fully. Why? Because they don't allow themselves to feel their own emotions. They remain distant and detached from them and are unable to put them into their characters. Are you one of those writers? Do you find it difficult to express your feelings, let alone feel them? I'm going to show you how to approach your own emotions as well as your characters' emotions.

You'll need to work on your characters from the inside to discover what type of emotions are residing behind their smiling faces. I once consulted with a man who was writing a novel about the love affair of an older couple. His basic problem had to do with the characters. They were stilted in their dialogue, flat in their feelings, and empty in their emotions. He wasn't able to put feelings into his characters, so I asked him about his own feelings.

Luckily, he was able to recall his emotions and began to inject them into his characters. His characters became so much richer and emotionally deep, that he ended up rewriting the beginning of his novel because he'd created unemotional characters.

What I learned from working with him was that until you can access your own emotions, you'll never be able to give emotions to your characters. By asking yourself probing questions, you will eventually retrieve your emotional memories. You'll be free to put your emotional honesty into all your characters and make them come alive by giving them an emotional reality—yours.

One caution: Make sure you don't write overly emotional stories filled with false feelings and sentimental characters. Think of soap operas, which are often written with overly emotional characters who are melodramatic and engage in exaggerated emotional responses. You don't want your readers or viewers to laugh instead of cry when your characters are having a heart-felt moment packed with emotion. Avoid writing maudlin characters and sentimental stories. You want to create characters who your readers can connect with while bringing their own emotions into the story.

EXERCISE

Growing Emotions From the Inside Out

Before you start to create your characters, ask these questions: "What do I want my characters to feel in this scene?" "What emotion do I want them to display?" "What would I feel in the same circumstances?"

Do you have a clear vision of the emotional life you want for your characters? Were you able to answer all of these questions? If yes, then you're well on the way to creating successful characters. Be sure to answer these questions so you'll know how your characters feel before you create them. Then you'll succeed in putting emotions into your characters.

In Janet Fitch's *White Oleander*, Astrid describes the difference in her mother's emotions after she meets Barry, who becomes her lover:

Passion. I never imagined it was something that could happen to her. These were days she couldn't recognize herself in a mirror, her eyes black with it, her hair forever tangled and smelling of musk, Barry's goat scent. . . .

Passion ruled her. Gone were the references to his physical goatishness, his need for dental work, his flabby physique, his squalid taste in clothes, the wretchedness of his English, his shameless clichés, the criminal triteness of his oeuvre, a man who wrote "snuck." . . . I watched her close her eyes, I could feel the waves of her passion like perfume across the teacups.

If you have no idea how to give your characters emotions, start with yourself and your emotions, exploring all the wonderful raw materials that are buried inside.

Do you feel passionate about the story you're writing? Do you feel emotionally connected to your characters and their feelings? Sometimes you can be too emotionally involved with your characters, which can prevent you from having the objectivity needed to create good characters. This has happened with writers I've worked with who have wanted to write about something too personal too soon, like the death of their lover or their latest divorce. They weren't able to do it objectively because their pain was too raw. If you want to write about an emotional event, you need to have enough emotional distance so that you're able to write about it with a level of objectivity. ■ ■ ■

EXERCISE
Expressing Emotions

What emotions do you want to express through your characters? Can you verbalize the emotions you want them to feel? Are these emotions that you're able to feel? Do you express these emotions? Can you readily identify them? It is imperative for you to answer these questions honestly if you want to create emotional characters who ring true to your audience.

You may avoid tapping your inner feelings and resist getting in touch with your own emotions. If you do, your characters will remain one-dimensional and stereotypical, preventing you from selling your writing. No matter how talented you are, until you're willing to ex-press yourself without fear and to reveal what you feel, your charac-ters will remain flat. If you can't release your emotions into your char-acters, they won't succeed. ▧ ▧ ▧

Emotions 101: Sad, Bad, Mad, Glad

Feel the feeling. —*Charles Rumberg*

Recently, I worked with a writer who developed exciting plots for her novels but her characters remained cold and unemotional. She was so removed from her feelings that she looked at me quizzically when I asked, "How did that make you feel?" She was great at writing mystery novels, but her writing dealt only with external conflicts and didn't include emotional relationships. Even though her plots and characters were filled with twists and turns, they lacked heart and spirit.

As we worked together, I discovered she was totally detached from her emotions because as a child she was punished whenever she showed anger or sadness. She learned to survive in her family by not expressing any emotions and burying the ones she did feel.

How can you successfully create emotional characters if you hide from your own emotions and don't know what you're feeling? First, become acquainted with your own emotions starting with four basic, universal ones. Let's call this Emotions 101.

The four basic emotions to start with are sad, bad, mad, glad. Every time you can't respond to "How did that make you feel?" choose one of these four emotions to help you focus on your feelings. "Does it make you feel Sad? Bad? Mad? Glad?"

You'll soon begin to connect to your feelings to these simple words, which from here on out, I'll refer to as SBMG. This emotional process will elevate your writing to another level of competence as you begin to infuse your characters with these emotions.

EXERCISE

Writing and Revealing Realistic Emotions

PART ONE: For the first part of this exercise, think about a recent personal situation in which you felt one of the four basic emotions mentioned above. Now, write a separate scene for each emotion, and remember to write with your senses (touch, taste, sound, sight and smell) and your heart.

After you've written about all four separate emotions, read each scene aloud to someone. What do you feel as you read each scene? Are you moved by what you've written? Do you understand the need to first feel the emotion before you put the feelings into your characters?

PART TWO: For the second part of this exercise, write four separate scenes using the same four basic emotions, only this time write them for your fictional characters. As I said earlier, by creating emotional characters who exhibit these core feelings, you're letting the reader identify with them without explicitly telling readers how to feel.

Also remember that the goal is to *show* these emotions through their actions, dialogue, and nonverbal expressions. For example, don't write, "Jane was feeling so mad, because her little brother didn't listen to her and was being bad. Yet, she was glad that he wasn't able to make her sad enough to cry." Show Jane feeling mad by having her slam the door as she picks up the dirty clothes he has thrown all over the room. Let action and dialogue express your character's emotions.

After you've finished writing four scenes with those emotions, read them aloud to yourself. How do your characters reveal their emotions?

Through action? Dialogue? Exposition? Are you able to identify what they're feeling? Are they experiencing the same emotions you felt when you wrote about yourself? Is there truth to what they're feeling or does it seem false? Are you characters' emotions believable?

Remember, if you can't move your readers or viewers to laugh, cry, scream, or tremble you won't have succeeded in creating characters worth caring about. When you write from the heart, your characters will tug at the hearts of your audience. ▪ ▪ ▪

Expressing Appropriate Emotions

> The only negative feelings are the ones that we can't accept within ourselves. —*Anita Johnston*

How many times a day are you involved with emotional conflicts that affect your mood? For example, what do you feel when your boss berates you? Anger? Shame? Hurt? Insecurity? What are your feelings when a friend ignores you? How do you relate to your mate when you both disagree? Do you shout or give her the silent treatment? Do you stomp out of the room? What do you do when someone you love is ill? Do you feel helpless or hopeless? Or do you feel scared and resentful?

You have to confront your emotions on a daily basis—at work, in love, in relationships, with family, and within yourself. How you act and react depends on how you were acculturated by your parents and taught to either express or ignore your emotions. This is especially true when it comes to the different ways girls and boys are taught to react by their parents. Boys and girls are still raised differently, even with all the advances women have made in the last century.

As a woman, how do you behave when you become angry? Were you told to control your emotions? How do you express your anger? Or are you not able to express your anger because you were told it's not nice for young ladies to get angry, that it's not ladylike to yell or scream? Girls are still taught not to act like tomboys or to show any aggression. But it's perfectly all right for girls to cry and show their tears when they're upset. Many women writers find it difficult to express anger and aggression through their characters because they've never learned how to express their own angry feelings in their relationships and in their lives. So their fictional male and female characters can be very ineffectual when showing stronger emotions.

As a man how do you behave when you're feeling hurt or sad? Do you show your feelings by crying or expressing your pain or do you cover them up and keep a stiff upper lip? While growing up, many males are told, "Big boys don't cry." Many psychologists maintain that as long as boys aren't allowed the freedom to express their sad feelings, there's a possibility these bottled up emotions will express themselves through violence and rage.

Since boys' aggressions are more acceptable to their parents than their vulnerable feelings, it's often difficult for male writers to express tender or sad emotions through their characters.

To reach full potential as an emotional writer, it's necessary for men to get in touch with their more vulnerable emotions and for women to accept their anger and aggressive nature.

The most important character traits you can give to all of your characters is make them real emotional human beings who bleed when they're cut and who cry when they're hurt. You want to create characters who have layers of emotions that are revealed throughout your story. You might begin with a character who is frightened and as he goes on a journey, you reveal signs of his courage little by little, until at the end of your story, your character fully reveals his courageous side. In other words, you have your characters change gradually. Peel the layers from your characters to find their truth, much as you peel the layers of an onion.

You can reveal your characters' feelings through conflict, through putting them under pressure and watching how they act and react. Successful characters are capable of being real, of feeling strong emotions and moving the audience to identify with them. Your audience connects to and identifies with your characters, because emotions create a state of excitement. Use strong feelings to propel your characters' behavior toward a specific goal.

Positive and Negative Emotions

It is the mind that maketh good or ill, That maketh wretch or happy, rich or poor. —*Edmund Spenser*

In life, you experience both positive and negative, pleasant and unpleasant emotions. It's important to call upon the different aspects of your own emotions—both the positive and the negative—to create emotional conflicts in your characters' personalities and relationships.

Breaking your emotions down into positive and negative ones will help you identify them in a more direct way and enable you to inject your characters with feelings when you want to write about a specific emotion.

Here are some emotions that are more targeted to specific moods:

Positive Emotions		*Negative Emotions*	
joy	tenderness	hate	suspicion
hope	fondness	shame	guilt
desire	excitement	worry	regret
love	curiosity	remorse	despair
surprise	happiness	fear	restlessness
calm	forgiveness	pity	anxiety
gratitude	festivity	rage	resentment
satisfaction	enthusiasm	loneliness	confusion
optimism	lightheartedness	jealousy	aggression
inspiration	playfulness	apathy	disgust

Now that you've mastered Emotions 101, let's focus on more spe-

FIRE AND ICE

Poetry is the spontaneous overflow of powerful feelings; it takes its origin from emotion recollected in tranquility.
—William Wordsworth

To help writers create characters who are emotional and real, I've devised what I refer to as the I.C.E. Method. Every character in a scene, story, or vignette needs I.C.E., which stands for intensity, conflict, and emotion. So many writing books stress structure, which is necessary, but writing really has to be emotional or it won't engage the reader. Characters without heart won't captivate readers enough to establish an emotional connection. You want to move your audience, to make them laugh, cry, rage, and feel. You only can do this by touching your audience through the characters' intensity, conflict and emotion.

Once, I worked with a novelist who had the proper story structure, great dialogue, a clear plot, but his characters were boring. Why? Because the characters were cold, unemotional, and dull. What his characters needed in the novel was I.C.E. He had to make the characters more intense, more conflicted, and more emotional. The story was there, but the characters weren't.

No matter how well structured your novel or script, without emotional characters in conflict your audience won't care. Now, this doesn't mean that you have to write about buildings blowing up or mutants taking over the water supply of the universe. A quiet scene can be intense, a scene between a child and his father can be emotional, and a love scene can be filled with conflict. Making a scene emotional and interesting is a matter of putting your feelings into your characters and giving them heat.

By tweaking your feelings and putting them into your characters, you'll give your characters I.C.E., which makes your audience feel F.I.R.E.

I added the word F.I.R.E., using a title from the Robert Frost poem "Fire and Ice." I've taken these two words and created an acronym for you to use with every new character you develop. F.I.R.E. is what you want your audience to feel every time you put I.C.E. into your characters:

FIRE AND ICE

Fear for your characters	Intensity
Identify with your characters	Conflict
Root for your characters	Emotions
Empathize with your characters	

Writing With F.I.R.E. and I.C.E.

Start with I.C.E., and create a character who has intensity, conflict, and emotion. Ask yourself if your characters make your readers feel F.I.R.E.? Do your readers feel *fear* for your characters? Do they *identify* with your characters? Do they *root* for your characters? Do they empathize with your characters? If you can answer yes, then you've accomplished a formidable task in learning how to give your characters emotional depth. Once you've finished, improve each of your fictional characters by making certain each is filled with intensity, conflict, and emotions.

You give your characters more intensity, conflict, and emotions by giving them a goal that they *desperately have* to reach. The more desperate the goal, the more *intensity*. The more opposition or obstacles that stand in the way, the more *conflict*. The greater the inner desire to reach the goal, the greater the *emotions*. ❧

cific emotions. Being more specific in attributing exact emotions to your characters can make them much more interesting than the ordinary and overused emotional tags.

Too often writers use ambiguous or abstract emotions as emotional tags, for example, "She felt worried," or "He was upset." These terms don't specifically reveal what the character is really feeling. You want to use emotions that conjure a more concrete feeling, and you want to show how the character behaves in a certain emotional state. Again the axiom, "Show don't tell," certainly applies when demonstrating emotions.

EXERCISE
Emotions In Conflict

Take two of the positive emotions from the list above and inject them into two of your fictional characters. You'll discover how dealing with your characters' positive emotional state deepens your writing and shows positive characterization. Now take two of the negative emotions and inject them into a couple of your fictional characters. This time, you'll discover how lifelike your characters become when their underlying structure is a negative emotion.

After you've attributed specific emotions to your characters, create a scene in which your protagonist and antagonist are in emotional conflict. How do they react to each other? Is the conflict powerful and convincing?

Does assigning an emotional state to your characters in advance help you focus on their emotions? Is the conflict in the scene between your protagonist and antagonist exciting and emotionally intense? Did sparks fly between them? Are you able to identify what they're feeling without stating the emotions? Are their actions and dialogue consistent with their emotions? If not, rewrite the scene until your readers know exactly what your characters are feeling in a consistent and motivated way. By using these emotions as guides you'll be able to plan in advance the feelings you want to portray through your characters. ■ ■ ■

Internal and External Emotions

It is not easy to find happiness in ourselves, and it is not possible to find it elsewhere. —*Agnes Repplier*

When you begin creating characters for your story, both you and your characters go on a journey. It is an emotional journey because without emotions your characters aren't real—they're just puppets on a string. There is no other way of creating characters except by taking the journey into your self. By writing from this place, you'll discover new emotional states, and your fictional characters will speak with voices that have been silent for years. These voices give greater range to your fictional cast of characters, who end up with louder voices and more to say!

Basically, you're creating characters on two levels—the external self and the internal self. Just as you have many layers to your personality, so do your characters.

Let's take a look at another excerpt from Janet Fitch's *White Olean-der*. This following paragraph foretells the actions of the mother, Ingrid, who eventually kills her lover, Barry. She's beautiful on the outside and dangerous to men on the inside. Her daughter, Astrid, narrates her conversation with her mother. Notice how the excerpt below reveals Astrid's emotions without once using the phrase "I feel." The narration also works to foreshadow the unrest and trouble that's about to disrupt Astrid's life.

"Oleander time," [Ingrid] said. "Lovers who kill each other now will blame it on the wind." She held up her large hand and spread the fingers, let the desert dryness lick through. My mother was not herself in the time of the Santa Anas. I was twelve years old and I was afraid for her. I wished things were back the way they had been, that Barry was still here, that the wind would stop blowing. . . . The edge of her white kimono flapped open in the wind and I could see her breast, low and full. Her beauty was like the edge of a very sharp knife.

Just think of how many people you've judged by their outside appearance, only to discover how wrong you were after getting to know them better. Beauty can mask vengeance (as we just saw in the excerpt from *White Oleander*), and ugliness can mask grace, as in the case of the famous fictional character Cyrano de Bergerac. It takes time and shared experiences to know the real person beneath the mask. When you create characters for your story, be sure to consider the emotions you want to illustrate through your characters' actions and interactions.

EXERCISE

Charting an Emotional Journey

Think about people you have met and began a relationship with who turned out to be completely different after you got to know them. Maybe they smiled and were charming, while inside they were raging and filled with fury. Write the scene in which their true personality emerged through their emotions. Use first person, present tense, and all of your senses. Show us the change through actions and description.

Next write a scene based on one of these experiences using one of your fictional characters. Let her discover that one of her lovers or friends is completely different from what she'd thought. Create an argument between the two characters, and show the emotional change unfolding between them.

When you're writing a story with a beginning, middle, and end, you're also going through an emotional journey with a beginning, middle, and end. So, when you create a character, there are two stories always going on: the emotional story of the character and the plot story of the structure. Your inner voice is intimately connected to

your character's inner voice and in turn to the audience, enabling them to feel a range of emotions.

In all good writing, the character's emotional story is connected to the plot structure, and the two occur simultaneously. Since characters create the emotional conflict and the action emerges from the characters, they evolve from each other and are synergistic. As characters go through a journey, they are emotionally changed along the way, as their change and growth is not physical. If you stick with this simple—not simplistic—way of writing, and approach it from your characters' emotional life and their external goal, the story structure and your characters' growth will be consistent and believable. ▪ ▪ ▪

Suppressed Emotions

> I have a sense of these buried lives striving to come out through me to express themselves. —*Marge Piercy*

Many times you may feel resistant to revealing your emotions because you don't trust others to know how you're really feeling, and you don't want to be vulnerable. You might not want to open yourself to criticism or hurt, so you suppress your true feelings. You also may lack the confidence to expose your feelings to others. It's frightening to open yourself up.

When you're not aware of your emotions, you often suppress them. That means they are buried in your subconscious mind and you're not aware of them unless you bring them up to your awareness. Suppressed emotions may find outlets in physical aliments such as backaches, stomachaches, or headaches. These emotions can be revealed through slamming doors, clenching fists, rising blood pressure, grinding teeth, shedding tears, throwing temper tantrums, and committing acts of violence.

It's important for you to get in touch with your suppressed emotions and allow them to surface. Don't hide your anger, fear, lust, greed, or envy. Your feelings are the essence of who you are and you don't want to feel shame or guilt because all of your emotions aren't good ones. By expressing these feelings through your characters in your stories and injecting your emotions into your characters, you will be breathing life into your characters and giving them the emotional depth needed to motivate their behavior.

EXERCISE
Sources of Suppression

What emotions have your characters suppressed? What traumatic events or crises happened to your character in the past? How did your character act out his repressed emotions? Write a scene answering the above questions. Write about one of your characters and a past traumatic event she's suppressed. Next, write a scene showing your character acting out the negative emotions she's suppressed. Now write another scene and allow your character to express her suppressed emotions. How powerful is that scene? How emotional is your character? ■ ■ ■

Opposing Emotions and Contradictory Feelings

> **What does not kill me makes me stronger.**
>
> —*Johann Wolfgang von Goethe*

A conflicted character, like an conflicted individual, is always filled with contradictory feelings. Characters in fiction and film often have opposing emotions (e.g., "I'm jealous of her, but I shouldn't be because she's my best friend and I love her"), which cause them inner conflict and stress.

These opposing drives create frustration within you and within your characters. The conflicts are the basis of the internal obstacles put in your character's path to keep him from reaching his goal. They are inner conflicts that come from deep inside your character. Just as you have to deal with your own personal conflicts so does your fictional character have to deal with his personal conflicts to reach his goal.

You have to be aware of your own psychology and your own opposing emotions before you can reveal what is beneath your character's mask. Many people are afraid of their anger, others their sexuality, still others their vulnerable side. Yet, it is these very opposing feelings that create more conflict between your characters and inside them. We all have contradictory emotions; if we didn't, we wouldn't have any conflict in our lives and in our stories. These polarities in our personality create conflict within ourselves and with others as well. The following excerpt from Helen Fielding's *Bridget Jones's Diary* is a great example of a character (Bridget) being at odds with herself:

TUESDAY 3 JANUARY

130 lbs. (terrifying slide into obesity—why? why?), alcohol units 6 (excellent), cigarettes 23 (v.g.), calories 2472.

9 a.m. Ugh. Cannot face thought of going to work. Only thing which makes it tolerable is thought of seeing Daniel again, but even that is inadvisable since am fat, have spot on chin, and desire only to sit on cushion eating chocolate and watching Xmas specials.

It is clear that Bridget is conflicted by her weight and has feelings of low self-esteem. She'd like to be thinner yet uses fattening food and alcohol to comfort herself. She displays these opposing emotions in her diary.

EXERCISE

Emotional Contradictions

Create a contradictory feeling in your character and write a scene showing your character reacting to the opposite emo-

tions. Did the scene have a lot of conflict? Was your character able to resolve her opposing feelings? Write about a character who desperately wants to achieve a goal and who can't because of a quality which prevents her from reaching it. ■ ■ ■

Your Character's Emotional Transformation

It takes a lot of courage to release the familiar and seemingly secure, to embrace the new. —*Alan Cohen*

In any good story, your main character has one emotion in the beginning of your story and throughout the emotional journey changes little by little as he overcomes obstacles and resolves conflicts. By the end of the story, his change and personal growth are believable because he has been motivated throughout the story. His emotional transformation from beginning to end is credible. It's important for you to know in advance how you want your character to emotionally change and transform. You need to know this even before you begin writing your story; otherwise, how can you motivate your character's behavior if you don't know what direction he is headed in?

You can't start with a character who has one emotion, and who abruptly changes to another one at the end of the story. Nobody would believe this because you haven't created motivation that causes the change. Haven't you read stories and seen films where the characters have suddenly changed without any motivation for the change? You might read about a character who is cold and distant, and then who suddenly becomes warm and loving in the end. The entire story would fail simply because the important small steps that are necessary for your character to take throughout the story don't exist.

You have to devise scenes and events for your characters to overcome and have them change in small but believable increments. It may sound simple to motivate your characters to change emotionally, but it's one of the hardest things to achieve. You want to have your characters struggle throughout their journey to eventually transform in the end.

A powerful example of a character's emotional transformation is Nora in Henrik Ibsen's play *A Doll's House.* Nora starts out as a dutiful, loving wife to Torvald Helmer who considers her his "little bird." Throughout the play, she begins to change and grow. At one point toward the end of the play, her husband tells Nora how much she needs his guidance:

HELMER: You loved me as a wife should love her husband. It was only the means that, in your inexperience, you misjudged. But do you think I love you the less because you cannot do without guidance? No, no. Only lean on me; I will counsel you, and guide you. I should be no true man if this very womanly helplessness did not make you doubly dear in my eyes. You mustn't dwell upon the hard things I said in my first moment of terror, when the world seemed to be tumbling about my ears. I have forgiven you, Nora—I swear I have forgiven you.

As they continue their discussion, Nora's transformation becomes evident, and there's no going back to their old relationships. She is about to leave Torvald, and when she closes the door, it's a noise that's heard around the world.

HELMER: To forsake your home, your husband, and your children! And you don't consider what the world will say.

NORA: I can pay no heed to that. I only know that I must do it.

HELMER: This is monstrous! Can you forsake your holiest duties in this way?

NORA: What do you consider my holiest duties?

HELMER: Do I need to tell you that? Your duties to your husband and your children.

NORA: I have other duties equally sacred.

HELMER: Impossible! What duties do you mean?

NORA: My duties towards myself.

HELMER: Before all else you are a wife and a mother.

NORA: That I no longer believe. I believe that before all else I am a human being, just as much as you are—or at least that I should try to become one. I know that most people agree with you, Torvald, and that they say so in books. But henceforth I can't be satisfied with what most people say, and what is in books. I must think things out for myself, and try to get clear about them.

Like Ibsen, each scene you write has to show the main character conquering an obstacle, which will provide him with the impetus for emotional change by the end of the story. For example, if your character starts out fearful, maybe he'll end up feeling courageous. Other examples could be going from insecure to secure, from weak to strong, from shy to outgoing, and from sad to happy.

Create momentum in your story by maintaining the character's goal, thus moving her forward to the end. Your readers will wonder, "Are they going to make it?" As the characters overcome obstacles, they start going through emotional and internal changes. You can't have characters without action, and you can't have action without characters. They are one and the same, and both simultaneously head toward resolution and transformation. Since the character's real story is the emotional story, it's important to have your main character experience an emotional transformational arc by the end of your story.

The Emotional Relationship

Why love if loving hurts so? —*C.S. Lewis*

In any good story there are emotional relationships between different characters. However, there should always be an emotional relationship between the main character and another major character. As a character goes on a journey, he is touched by different people, just as he touches them. The main character can have a number of emotional relationships, but the one major emotional relationship is the relationship that must be resolved by the end.

In the novel *Ordinary People*, by Judith Guest, Conrad, the son, has returned from a mental institution after he'd tried to kill himself after the accidental drowning of his brother from a boating accident. Although the accident wasn't Conrad's fault, he can't stop feeling guilt and responsibility for his brother's death.

Conrad is the main character and has relationships with his mother, his father, his brother, his coach, a girl in the mental hospital, a new girlfriend at school, his friends, and his psychiatrist. But it's Conrad's relationship with his mother that is the main emotional relationship in the story. Conrad desperately wants his mother's love, but in the end, he accepts that she's incapable of loving him. His emotional growth involves his realization that it's his mother who is emotionally unavailable and yet he loves her anyway. In the following excerpt, Beth and Cal, Conrad's mother and father are having a heated discussion about Conrad as he enters the room. As you read, notice how the descriptions of the characters and their actions convey the awkwardness and tension that exists between the family members. Even an excerpt as brief as this one is enough to illustrate the anguish of this emotional relationship:

Now [Conrad] stands on the stairs, as Cal comes back inside. "I'm going to bed," he says. "See you in the morning."

"All through studying?" Cal asks.

He nods. "It's just a quiz in trig. Shouldn't be hard. I'm tired. It was sort of a rough week."

"What happened?" he asks. "Your grandmother give you a hard time?"

"No. Nothing like that. She was fine. I'm just—I'm glad you're back, that's all."

And he goes to *her,* then, without any hesitation; it is what he has come downstairs for, obviously. He bends his head, puts an arm around her in a quick, clumsy embrace.

"G'night." His voice is thick. He exits swiftly, his face turned away.

She sits on the couch, her legs curled under her, the book in her lap, just as he has left her. She is staring off into space. Then, after a moment, her head drops over her book again, her hair spilling over her shoulder. Her face is hidden from Cal, also.

EXERCISE

Writing for an Emotional Response

What reaction do you want your audience to have? Create characters who fulfill your audience's expectations emotionally. Write about characters in a pressure cooker, who can grow emotionally as you peel away the layers of their personality. Write a scene about your character starting with one emotional state and ending up with another. Show the change and make it dramatic and believable. ■ ■ ■

Mining Your Emotional Depths

I learned never to empty the well of my writing, but always
to stop when there was still something there in the deep part

of the well, and let it refill at night from the springs that
fed it. —*Ernest Hemingway*

The truly great artists are those who are able to reveal their innermost feelings. Writing from this place is what creates characters who matter and with whom everyone can identify. To show the truth or honesty in your characters, you must go down to your deepest core by becoming aware of what you feel and by monitoring your feelings. If you accept your emotional self, then you'll be able to describe what you're feeling through your characters.

The importance of your relationship to the characters you invent reflects the deletion of your self-consciousness. Loss of the self becomes evident when you let your emotions flow into your characters. You are one and the same, and you need to have an emotional relationship to your characters and no longer be separate from them. It is often what successful athletes refer to as being in the "zone," a state in which you aren't aware of anything around you because you're completely immersed in what you're doing. In your case that means breathing life into your characters.

If your ego intrudes when you're writing characters, it interferes with your creative energy. After you have a basic foundation for your character, you can ask yourself if the character has the emotional spine you need for your story. After you find the core or essence of your character, you can attach emotions to his essence. But be sure you don't start analyzing too soon—you don't want to lose your creative flow.

Writing from your emotions is not being sentimental or self-indulgent. When you start to create characters who come alive, you need to be selective with the emotions you give them, rather than letting all your feelings hang out. You must go beyond the sentimental. Follow your feelings, and go deeper and deeper inside. Stretch yourself, and write out of the parameters of your inner being. Write from those unconscious places where you usually are afraid to go.

Being an Emotional Writer

Write your heart out. —*Bernard Malamud*

Commit yourself to excavating the feelings deep inside yourself, and put them into your characters. If you know you can enter places where feelings are hidden and yet leave them when it's over, you are beginning to trust yourself. You must begin to have a sense of yourself as the creator of characters when you look at your past. Trust yourself in order to create honest characters with real feelings. When you access your feelings, accept rather than censor them. Use your emotional life as a road map for your characters' emotional life. Embrace all of your emotions so that they'll be available to your characters, and let them create tension and suspense in your stories.

There is freedom in acknowledging and honoring your own emotions. No one else in your life is going to do it for you! Through creating characters, you'll find compassion for who you are and for what you're feeling. Give your childhood respect. Be kind to yourself. Honor your feelings. Your being that lives inside you is your source of creative energy and of universal characters. It flows through you and through your art to connect with others. It is your essence. As you embrace being an emotional writer, you must find joy in writing from this deeper space.

Writing is a lifestyle of its own. Tapping into your inner world and your character's inner world will allow you to create fascinating and complex characters. A depth experience in a good movie or book involves you and your audience feeling deep emotions. It should be your goal to write characters who move your readers and viewers—to touch their spirit and their hearts. This is what creates exciting characters.

coping with conflict: characters' defense mechanisms and masks

Men should be what they seem . . . —*William Shakespeare*

onflict is the strength of any exciting character and story. Without conflict, characters don't have drive, desire, or desperation. Without conflict, there's no story, just words. Conflict is one of the most important building blocks for exciting characters. Through conflict, your characters shed their layers bit by bit until we discover the different aspects of their hidden selves. The characters' internal conflicts create the dramatic action for your story.

This chapter will include various types of conflicts and the overt and covert reactions to conflict. You'll learn how to throw characters into the middle of conflict to give them momentum, tension, and suspense and to force them to take off their masks.

Emotions and Conflict

The Promised Land always lies on the other side of a wilderness. —*Havelock Ellis*

Emotional conflict is what all great characters carry inside and what all exciting writing must contain. Every story you write deals with characters in emotional conflict. It doesn't matter if you're writing a thriller, an action adventure, a period piece, or a romance novel, all the characters must be involved with emotional conflicts. That doesn't mean your plot can't have battles, riots, mayhem, terrorist attack,

129

wars, tornadoes, earthquakes, plane crashes, hurricanes, fires, floods, or famine. Yes, you can put all of these external conflicts in your story, but it's imperative for you to create characters with inner conflicts like fears, resentments, or frustrations.

Since all fiction writing needs to have emotional conflict, how do you develop it? First, you must give your main character a goal, and then put obstacles in the path of his goal. These obstacles are necessary to create both internal and external conflict for the character. The greater the obstacles and complications, and the more hurdles your main character has to overcome, the more powerful and absorbing your conflict and story become.

Even if your character doesn't reach his goal, he still has to struggle toward it. Otherwise, there is no conflict and without conflict, there is no drama. Fear is one of the most overriding emotions that fictional characters can face. Fear is a basic emotion and the cause of both inner and outer conflicts. So if you want to create emotional conflict for your characters, fear is a good candidate to deal with.

In John D. MacDonald's *The Executioners* (also known as the movie *Cape Fear)*, a prosecutor, Sam Bowden, and his family are suddenly invaded by a terrifying ex-con, Max Cady, who blames Bowden for sending him to jail.

The entire family becomes permeated by fear when Cady makes subtle threats, kills the family dog, and stalks the Bowdens.

Fear of the unknown is the basic emotion throughout the story. MacDonald's novel shows how fear suddenly makes a grown man unravel, as he becomes obsessed with the safety of his wife and children against a cunning, evil killer who is out for vengeance. Bowden's fear is responsible for his emotional downward spiral into what lengths he'll go to stop Cady—even if it means he has to kill him.

What do your characters want desperately enough to motivate them into taking action and to move the story to its climax? To achieve the ultimate conflict for your characters ask, "What would my characters fight for, and what would they die for?"

Inherent in the answers to these questions is the necessity of creating powerful, emotional conflicts. There are many different types of conflict, and you can make use of one or more of them to establish suspense, emotion, and excitement in your characters.

Action vs. Emotional Conflict

The gem cannot be polished without friction, nor man perfected without trials. —*Confucius*

Writing is all about conflict. But I'm not talking just about violence, armies, or wars. You must also fill your stories with your character's inner conflict to build tension and suspense. Good storytelling involves human emotions that will make your readers and viewers emotionally involved.

The success of action films or suspense novels not only has to do with suspense, twists, turns, surprise, and shock—all necessary elements in these stories—but also with emotional conflict. In novels such as *The English Patient* or *Gone With the Wind*, it is the emotional conflict between the male and female characters and not the conflicts of war that move and involve the audience. Director James Cameron gave us the lovers, Rose and Jack, in his film *Titanic* because he was wise enough to know that dealing with his lovers would allow the audience to intimately experience their plight because of their love, rather than feel emotional about a sinking ship. Action novels and films which fail are those that only have action conflict but haven't connected to the audience in any deep way.

You can create characters who are in conflict in armies, wars, disasters, and even involved in the ultimate conflict—death. However, unless you focus on the emotional conflicts of your main and major characters, these other conflicts will have little emotional impact.

Think of how you've reacted in the past to novels or films that

were filled with relentless, nonstop conflict. As you witnessed massive beatings, wars, and chaos, you weren't involved, and you became insensitive to all these massive conflicts. It wasn't because you're a cold, unfeeling person; it was that you weren't emotionally attached to any of the characters. In a story where you're emotionally connected to specific characters, you're more moved by them having an argument than you are watching men fight and die.

Types of Conflict

Remember, a kite rises against—not with—the wind.
—Hamilton Mabie

Three basic sources of conflict are found within most great novels, as well as throughout history. The pitting of man against himself, man against nature, and man against man. Each of these opens the door for both internal and external obstacles that your characters must face—for better or for worse. Whether he succeeds or fails, he'll inevitably have undergone a mental, possibly even physical change that affects his reasoning, his actions, and his long-term motivations. Let's explore each of these a bit more.

Man Against Himself

It's a sad day when you find out that it's not accident or time or fortune but just yourself that kept things from you.
—Lillian Hellman

Man against himself is one of the most important conflicts in fiction, as well as in life. Think of all the times you've had emotional conflicts because of internal warring emotions. How many New Year's resolutions did you make and eventually break? That's an example of emotional conflict within. You want to achieve something and your inner conflicts fight against the very thing you want to accomplish.

If you want to write a story about man against himself, you need to recall the times you vowed not to do something and ended up doing it, even if it was bad for you. This emotional conflict is evident in all addictive behavior. Addicts know that alcohol, food, drugs, sex, gambling, or other addictions are destructive to them.

Let's say that Adam, a young music producer, who is a cocaine addict, swears to himself and to others that he'll never use again. His addiction has lead to his arrest for possession of drugs. He's made bail and is out, but soon the craving seeps in and eventually hits him full force. He can't think of anything else except to give into his unstoppable urge.

The craving for instant gratification overpowers his desire to stop the addiction, and he caves into that relentless urge without looking at the consequences of his behavior. He throws caution to the wind and his future down the drain because of his addiction. Adam loses his job, his girlfriend leaves him, and he's arrested again. This time, he ends up with a one-year sentence for mandatory rehab.

Adam's emotional conflict is powerful and unstoppable. You can see that by creating characters who have inner emotional conflicts, you'll create characters whose struggle will create empathy in your readers and viewers. The greater the urge, the greater the internal turmoil and the greater the conflicts.

In the novel *Requiem for a Dream*, by Hubert Selby Jr., both the mother, Sara, and her son, Harry, spiral downward into a cloudy, confusing drug-induced world. Sara tries to lose weight and becomes hooked on prescription diet pills. Her son uses cocaine and heroin. Their drugs fill them with the possibility of realizing their dreams, but instead they're both living a nightmare.

There are also emotional conflicts that aren't as life threatening as drug addiction. For example, in Helen Fielding's *Bridget Jones's Diary*, Bridget is a neurotic heroine who chronicles her inner battles with

FATAL FLAWS

People only see what they are prepared to see.

—Ralph Waldo Emerson

In conflicts that show man against himself, you may also discover characters who are trying to overcome some internal emotional flaw. If you're writing a tragedy, the fatal flaw will be the downfall of your main character. The fatal flaw should always be planted within the character's personality in the beginning of your story, so that the ending is believable.

William Shakespeare wrote famous tragedies in which the hero suffered from a fatal flaw like jealousy, insecurity, or the need for power or revenge. Some of his most well-known heroes with fatal flaws are Othello (jealousy), Hamlet (revenge), and Macbeth (power). Remember that a fatal flaw is inherent in the character, and ultimately causes the downfall of that character. In a tragedy, that usually means death.

The following emotional flaws can function as fatal flaws:

Frustration	Fear
Apprehension	Loneliness
Terror	Anger
Anguish	Worry
Loathing	

The protagonist can overcome such fatal flaws, possibly when her blinders are removed and she can understand her emotional problem. For example, in Anna Quindlen's novel *One True Thing*, the daughter, Ellen, who has always worshipped her father, leaves her job and returns home to take care of her cancer-stricken mother. As her mother's caregiver, Ellen discovers wonderful qualities about her mother that both she and her father had always taken for granted.

She discovers she has perceived her parents incorrectly, and as a result, she and her mother are able to rebuild their mother-daughter relationship before her mother's death. ↔

self-acceptance, her weight, her drinking, her smoking, and her poor taste in men. In this excerpt from *Bridget Jones's Diary*, you can see that her major source of conflict is her own self:

> On way home in end-of-Christmas denial I bought a packet of cut-price chocolate tree decorations and a 3.69 [pounds sterling] bottle of sparkling wine from Norway, Pakistan or similar. I guzzled them by the light of the Christmas tree, together with a couple of mince pies, the last of the Christmas cake and some Stilton, while watching Eastenders, imagining it was a Christmas special.
>
> Now, though, I feel ashamed and repulsive. I can actually feel the fat splurging out from my body. Never mind. Sometimes you have to sink to a nadir of toxic fat envelopment in order to emerge, phoenix-like, from the chemical wasteland as a purged and beautiful Michelle Pfeiffer figure.

Man Against Nature

Life seems to be a never-ending series of survivals . . .
—*Carroll Baker*

You can see the conflict of man against nature in action-packed adventure movies and novels such as *Alien, Jurassic Park,* and *Planet of the Apes.* The main character's goal is always thwarted by some act of nature that almost prevents him from reaching his goal. These struggles usually involve life and death issues. Will your characters survive the erupting volcano, the dinosaur, or the killer bees?

A classic example of the man against nature conflict can be found in Ernest Hemingway's *The Old Man and the Sea.* The old man, Santiago, is a fisherman who has to test his physical strength as well as his strength of character as he battles an eighteen-foot Marlin alone. It's an exciting tug-of-war conflict between Santiago and the Marlin for survival.

EXERCISE

Conflicts in Nature

Recall a situation in which you interacted with nature in a way that created conflict. Were you lost in the woods? Did you have a scare with an animal? Were you in a blizzard? A fire or flood? An earthquake? Write about the scene with all of your senses, and put the feelings you experienced into the scene. Even if your experience with nature wasn't a major conflict, you certainly can use it to create an exciting character in conflict with nature. ■ ■ ■

Man Against Man

When it comes to the pinch, human beings are heroic.

—*George Orwell*

The most popular type of conflict involves man against man. In this type of conflict, the main character has a goal and another character stands in the way of him reaching his goal. You can find this conflict in mystery, spy, detective, and war stories. But the most dramatic type of conflict with man against man is the small personal story involving families, lovers, friends, and relationships. Examples include *Ordinary People, American Beauty,* and *The Great Santini.* These stories involve man against man in an emotional and psychological way, rather than in a good against evil way. These personal conflicts include family members struggling with themselves and with one another. They are powerful because they are universal, and your readers and viewers can and will identify with them.

When you create characters who experience man against man conflicts, you have to build the conflicts within the character in a greater way than you would if you were creating characters who are in a mystery or a plot-oriented story.

In all good writing, the main character and other characters should always have internal conflicts, along with the other types of conflicts.

The most powerful writing involves both internal and external conflicts. You want your characters to feel torn by their emotional conflicts and hopefully resolve them by the end, while also resolving the plot.

Personal stories have more impact on your audience than the greatest car crash could ever have. Tobias Wolff wrote *This Boy's Life*, an autobiography about his relationship with his mean step-father and the emotional and psychological conflicts the relationship created. How Wolff coped and eventually broke free from his abusive step-father shows readers the emotional conflicts of a young boy, who eventually transformed and overcame his emotional adversity as well as his living adversary.

EXERCISE
Avoiding or Confronting Conflicts

Write a scene with your character in conflict with himself because of internal conflicts. Now create another scene with the same character (the protagonist) in conflict with another character (the antagonist). If you are able to, try and use a personal or childhood experience to write this scene.

Many times we're forced into conflict whether we like it or not, and we have to confront it. If you want to create exciting characters who don't avoid conflicts and who are active and strong, you will have to face your own fear of conflict in order to become a writer whose stories are filled with characters confronting conflicts head on. ▪ ▪ ▪

EXERCISE
Coping With Conflicts

What happens when you face conflict in your life? How do you react? This is an important question because the way you react to conflict is often the way you show your characters reacting. Can you show your anger? Are you able to be sad and vulnerable and let others know how you feel? Do you always feel like a victim in conflict? Do all your characters sound like victims? Can you give your

characters angry emotions? Write a scene in which your main character expresses anger. ▣ ▣ ▣

Sources of Conflict

Great deeds are usually wrought at great risk. —*Herodotus*

Opposing emotional drives create conflict and frustration within hu-
mans and within characters. These frustrations result from obstacles
in your character's path that keep him from reaching his goal. Inner
conflicts come from deep frustration within your character. Just as
you have to deal with your own personal conflicts, so do your fictional
characters deal with their personal conflicts.

Frustrations occur when a person is prevented from reaching a
positive goal or avoiding a negative goal. Frustration is a very basic
response to feeling thwarted, blocked, or trapped in negative relationships or situations in which you see no clear way out. These are innate
and fundamental reactions to not getting your needs met. Even small
babies will become aggressive and throw tantrums when their needs
aren't met and they become frustrated.

The two basic types of frustration are environmental and personal.
Environmental frustration has to do with such circumstances as lack
of money, parental restrictions, lack of housing, lack of food, societal
restrictions, physical restrictions, and terrorism. Personal frustration
includes inadequate intelligence, disease, physical handicaps, lack of
physical strength, mental illness, emotional conflicts, and psychological disturbances. When you create characters, give them either environmental or personal frustrations in order to intensify the level of
conflict in your story.

Reactions to Conflict

He conquers who endures. —*Perseus*

The two direct responses to frustration are either fight or flight. Every day you may employ aspects of the fight or flight reaction to frustration and stress in your life. Your characters also use these reactions to fear.

Fighting usually involves some type of destructive physical act that escalates and leads to further conflict. Gunfights, duels, brawls, or fist-fights represent direct reactions to frustrations and conflicts. There are also more indirect ways of fighting, which include verbal abuse such as blaming, arguing, criticism, sarcasm, name calling, and barbed threats.

Flight is also a direct reaction to frustration and includes actions such as running away, hiding, quitting, leaving home, and ending relationships. The more common methods of using flight against frustrations are indirect actions of tuning out through daydreams, fantasies, disinterest, apathy, detachment, and even suicide. James Thurber wrote a wonderful story called "The Secret Life of Walter Mitty," which demonstrates how a man flees from the humdrum of his daily life through his fantasies.

Another way of reacting to frustration is self-sabotage, which is an indirect response to the flight instinct. When frustrated or conflicted, an individual might turn his frustrations inward against himself and drive recklessly or take excessive drugs to escape his emotional pain.

Since all novels, shorts stories, or scripts are about characters in conflict, let's look at the some of the patterns of conflict you can use for your characters.

Patterns of Conflict

There is no sense in the struggle, but there is no choice but to struggle. —*Ernie Pyle*

The patterns of conflict listed below demonstrate the problems that come from having to make decisions that create conflict and frustration in the individuals:

Double-approach conflicts cause the individual to choose between two goals. They both could be positive goals like getting married or moving to another city for a career promotion. Most stories involve this type of conflict, where in the end the main character has to make a choice between love or career; moving to another town or staying; going back to school or staying in her job. In all cases, neither decision leads to dire consequences, but the choice still may be difficult to make if the character desires both equally.

For example, in the film *When Harry Met Sally*, Harry falls in love with Sally, but he is torn between commitment and freedom. While neither choice is inherently bad, they both present problems and conflicts.

Double-avoidant conflicts are more painful because the character has to choose between two negative goals. In Anna Quindlen's *Black and Blue*, the wife must choose between staying with her husband and getting physically abused, or leaving him and going underground with her son. If she leaves she'll be giving up her family, friends, job, and identity, and making her son leave his father. If she stays, she's afraid her husband will abuse her and eventually kill her. Both conflicts have painful consequences.

Approach-avoidant conflicts are decisions that involve choosing what you believe to be a pleasurable goal but which later leads to suffering and painful consequences. For example, a character who can't cope with her anxiety might choose to drink too much to calm her nerves. In the long run, this choice creates more pain for her and she could become an alcoholic. If your character suffers from anxiety and chooses not to turn to alcohol to calm her, that is another choice.

These types of conflicts usually involve individuals suffering from addictions. In Rebecca Wells's *Divine Secrets of the Ya-Ya-Sisterhood*, Sidda Walker's mother, Vivi Walker, drinks too much, and does and says outlandish things, especially to her daughter. Vivi uses alcohol to avoid facing her own reality and for immediate gratification.

In all stories, characters must make choices and decisions. The majority of their frustrations lead to conflict resolution by the end of

the story. The characters deal with their frustration by taking direct
or indirect actions involving fight or flight. These can be as innocuous
as the silent treatment or as dangerous as killing another person.

Defense Mechanisms

**What we call "normal" is a product of repression, denial, split-
ting, projection, introjection and other forms of destructive
actions on experience. —***R.D. Laing*

Defense mechanisms are unconscious attempts of a person to protect
himself against threats to the integrity of the ego and to relieve tension
and anxiety resulting from unresolved frustrations and conflicts.
Deeply rooted frustrations and conflicts that can't be resolved lead
the individual to develop defense mechanisms. Sigmund Freud considered defense mechanisms to be a set of psychological devices by
which the ego distorts the perception of reality to protect the individual, thus allowing the person to achieve a sort of mental and emotional
balance.

It has been formulated that people with high self-esteem can accept
and adjust to frustration and stress better than individuals with lower
self-esteem who are easily threatened and need to protect their self-
image by developing defense mechanisms. The following are some
common defense mechanism:

1. **Compensation:** You strive for perfectionism by overcompensat-
   ing for weaknesses—real or imagined. For example, a child gets
   all As in school or excels at sports, because she doesn't feel good
   about herself.

2. **Conversion:** You have an overwhelming sense of fear that manifests itself as a physical or mental disability. For example, GIs
   in war can suddenly become blind or crippled because they
   couldn't save a buddy or hid in fear during a battle.

3. **Denial:** You don't deal with frustration directly, but focus in-

stead with other less painful issues. For example, a man in a dire financial situation may gamble on a football game instead of making a late house payment.

4. **Identification:** You lose a sense of self and begin to identify with those in control or power. For example, victims of kidnappings can begin to identify with their kidnappers so much so that they don't even try to escape.

5. **Projection:** You protect yourself by putting bad traits onto another person who reminds you of these same undesirable traits in yourself. Projection involves not liking things about another person that you don't like in yourself but refuse to accept.

6. **Repression:** You exclude from consciousness or memory an event that is too painful to deal with. Individuals repress desires, impulses, and feelings that are psychologically disturbing or arousing. However, such events or desires may continue to exist in the unconscious. For example, a priest who has sexual desires may be subconsciously motivated to preach about the dangers of sin and immorality.

7. **Suppression:** Unlike repression, suppression is when you consciously engage to control unacceptable feelings and impulses. For example, you feel sexual toward a stranger, you suppress these feelings rather than act upon them.

8. **Undoing:** When you feel guilty about something you've done, you try to make up for it through gifts or acts of kindness. In *Divine Secrets of the Ya-Ya Sisterhood,* both the mother and daughter have emotional outbursts at each other and then call or send presents to try and make up. When Vivi is a young mother and feels guilty, she tries to undo her outbursts by being especially nice to Sidda.

9. **Sublimation:** This is when you channel unacceptable feelings into other strong socially acceptable activities such as volunteer-

ing in a hospital or donating money to the homeless.

10. **Compulsive-obsessive behaviors:** You escape frustrations through outside distractions and develop coping mechanisms through repetitive behaviors, such as constantly washing your hands, cleaning the house, or checking the electrical sockets over again and again. A good example of a character with compulsive-obsessive behavior is the character played by Jack Nicholson in the film *As Good As It Gets*. Most of his behavior is so compulsive that he is unable to get along with anyone. He locks and relocks his front door, avoids stepping on sidewalk cracks, and follows specific rituals when he enters his home or eats out at restaurants.

11. **Rationalization:** You make excuses for other people or yourself. We substitute perfectly normal reasons for our behavior because the real reasons are unacceptable to our conscious self. For example, a woman who stays married to a man who beats her might rationalize that her children need a father, when in fact the real reason is she's afraid that she can't make it on her own.

12. **Addictions:** You engage in behaviors that are compulsive, including addictions to drugs, alcohol, food, sex, gambling, or any behavior that reduces anxiety or frustration on a temporary basis and eventually stops working. These addictions lead to self-destruction. The solution to the original frustration and conflict eventually becomes the real problem.

Since all stories consists of characters in conflict, it's important for you to refer to these different types of defense mechanisms developed to protect one against conflict. Use specific defense mechanisms for your various characters. When you create realistic characters, give them different defense mechanisms. For example, you could have a character be in denial about her child's drinking. Or perhaps you could create a character who sublimates his sexual feelings for his teacher by getting on the honor roll.

EXERCISE
Developing Defense Mechanisms

Choose three defense mechanisms for your characters. Write three separate scenes involving each defense mechanism against frustration. Perhaps you can recall some of the defense mechanisms you've used in your life in the scene with your characters. Make your characters' defenses real and believable so your readers will empathize with them. ■ ■ ■

Protection From Conflict

The greatest gift you can give anyone is your honest self.

—*Fred Rogers*

You might have heard the saying, "Believe nothing of what you hear and half of what you see." That saying is applicable for your characters in that there's more to them than meets the eye. You and your characters are hiding secrets behind the myriad masks you wear. We develop our masks as another form of self-protection against getting hurt and being too vulnerable. Just as you can't judge a book by its cover, you can't judge a person by the way she acts or looks.

In the ancient Greek dramas, actors wore actual masks to play roles of the different characters in a play. They literally portrayed the facades of their characters through these masks. All of us wear masks in our own lives. We wear different masks for different people, situations, and relationships. Very few people get to know who we really are because we have many levels to our personalities and can decide in advance how we want to portray ourselves in certain situations.

All of your characters also wear protective masks. Throughout the course of the story, characters take off their masks when faced with different types of conflict.

Unfortunately, most of us can't reach our powerful emotions because we wear our protective masks most of the time. Our masks keep us alienated from our inner selves and from developing intimacy with others. Only in rare moments are we able to connect on a deep emotional level to another person. If we're lucky, we have a handful of family and close friends who get glimpses of our true selves. In fiction, connections happen between a parent and child, or between lovers.

We learn how to put on our masks by the time we're young children, when our parents scold us for being honest. Can you remember an incident when your parents yelled at you for expressing your true feelings or opinions about someone or something?

You might have been honest with your feelings and were just expressing your true emotions, but you were berated for doing that. After enough scolding, you learned to hide your true feelings behind a mask. Unfortunately, after doing this for too long, your true self becomes completely hidden.

We've been mocked by our peers, reprimanded by the church, disciplined by our parents, teachers, and relatives, and we learn to put on our protective mask and not be who we really are. Even though we're spontaneous and free when we're very young, we eventually learn to hide our true "self."

If you don't learn how to hide your feelings behind your mask, others will view you as strange or weird, and you won't be socially accepted. So you also wear your mask as a means of self-protection, which helps you from being too vulnerable or from getting hurt.

The problem is that many people also cut off their emotions and become detached from their feelings. They don't know who they are on the inside, and are only able to identify with their masks.

What matters in your stories is who your characters are without the outer masks they wear. Are you able to answer the question, "Who am I?" beneath your masks? Are you aware of the real you without a mask? How many masks do you wear? If you can't answer truthfully, then how can you unmask your fictional characters? You need to work on yourself first and become aware of all the masks you wear in your own life before you're able to take off your characters' masks.

To be a deeper writer, you must learn to separate yourself from the many masks you wear in life, work, and family. For now, you're going to remove your mask and write from the person you were meant to be. This is a very powerful way to write. It also helps you get beneath your persona or mask, and, in turn, get beneath your characters' masks to the real people inside.

F. Scott Fitzgerald's *The Great Gatsby* is filled with characters pretending to be people they aren't. When one character, Daisy Buchanan, is involved in a hit-and-run and kills a woman, Jay Gatsby, the man who loves her, takes the blame. In the end, the narrator Nick Carraway learns that even the wealthy Gatsby isn't the man he claimed to be—he actually made his money illegally. Like everyone else in the novel, Gatsby was striving to be someone he could never become by wearing a mask to the world.

EXERCISE
What Are Your Characters Hiding?

What are the masks your character wears? Does he wear the mask of a lawyer, a doctor, a clerk, a father, a husband, a lover, a son, a brother, a criminal?

What are the emotional masks your character wears? Does she have the facade of a victim, loser, winner, artist, mother? Write a scene in which your character wears a mask. Describe how other characters react. What pain or secrets is your main character hiding beneath the masks? What is it your character hopes to avoid?

Now write a scene when your character is forced to remove the mask. As you answer the above questions for your characters, you will be better able to understand their fears and emotions.

There are talented writers who may never reach their full potential because they are emotionally removed from this vast reservoir of feelings. Writers who've had success in creating deep and layered characters know the secret of being able to write beneath their own masks to connect with their inner emotions and to put them into their fictional characters. The free and open writer listens to and is attuned to his emotions, defenses, masks, and inner conflicts.

Creating fictional characters who originate from your inner characters and have similar problems to your own can give you the opportunity to practice for future actions you will take in your own life. I have seen many writers get more therapeutic benefits through writing than through therapy! ▪ ▪ ▪

Conflicts or Choices

> Destiny is not a matter of chance, it is a matter of choice; it
> is not a thing to be waited for, it is a thing to be achieved.
> —*William Jennings Bryan*

To be alive is to know conflict. Life is filled with conflicts as minor as which outfit to wear on a blind date or which entree to order in a restaurant. Such examples are usually considered to be choices rather than conflicts. In fiction, the characters' choices or decisions create the story, just as the choices you have made are responsible for the way your life is now. However, unlike the above examples, most choices aren't that easy.

We base our choices on past experiences, values, perceptions, attitudes, beliefs, and awareness. Many more unconscious aspects influence our choices. In fiction you need to build characters who make choices based on their backstory, inner motivation, and psychology so that their behavior is believable.

A Character's Persona: A Case Study of When Choice Becomes Conflict

**You gain strength, courage and confidence by every experience
in which you really stop to look fear in the face.**
—*Eleanor Roosevelt*

Let's suppose that you're writing a story about relationships, and you create a single woman in her early twenties who's a stockbroker. She's dynamic and gorgeous, and she knows how to charm men. She has no trouble attracting men, but she has no luck in maintaining long-term relationships with any of them. None of her past relationships have worked out, and unfortunately her lovers are the ones who dump her.

Why does this happen to such a beautiful woman? Why can't she sustain a relationship? Why do the men in her life leave her? What is it about her that drives them away? What's wrong with her? It certainly isn't that she's not beautiful or physically desirable to men. She certainly has the opportunity to meet men through her job. So what is the problem?

Let's suppose a new man comes into her life at work who is interested in dating her. She is attracted to him, but she's also conflicted when he asks her for a date. She's scared to get romantically involved again. She's been burned one too many times. In this situation, your character isn't just going to make an easy choice on whether or not to accept a date with this man. She's coming to this relationship with a past. She's been hurt by men, and she's been cheated on by them. Each man she has dated ended the relationship while she still loved him.

Of course, she doesn't look at herself as the problem. She doesn't become introspective to see if there is anything she's doing to drive her lovers away. She just feels hurt and a lack of trust when they break up with her.

In this situation, do you think the character will make clear-cut choices about starting a relationship? Her choices will be based on her past affairs, her fearful attitude toward men, her negative emotions about trusting any man, and not having ever experienced a loving relationship that ended in marriage.

Her choices are now colored by her unsuccessful experiences that created the inner conflicts. Her conflicting emotions confuse her. She is torn between her need for love and attention from the opposite sex and her fear of getting hurt. Her desire for love motivates her to finally go out on a date, and in spite of her fears, she is immediately smitten with the young man.

Now the character has to deal with her inner fears because she is once again vulnerable to a man. She still is wearing her smiling, confident persona, but inside she's worried about betrayal, pain, and fear. Her anxiety overwhelms her.

After only a few dates, she starts to act very needy. Instead of being the confident, beautiful woman he was initially attracted to, she now acts insecure and jealous. She starts asking him when she's going to see him again, when he's going to call, and what he did when he wasn't with her. Before long her confidant persona has disappeared because her feelings of insecurity and mistrust have become stronger than her facade.

She becomes more frustrated. On the one hand, she desperately wants love, and yet she's waiting to be hurt and disappointed again. She begins to imagine the worse case scenario—that her lover will lose interest and drop her. And that is exactly what happens, but not because he was bad or untrustworthy, but because she has driven him away with her unpredictable behavior, her suspicious nature, and her neediness.

After he drops her, she becomes even more needy and insecure, and her lack of self-esteem continues on a downward spiral until she is thoroughly bitter and cynical about men. What originally attracted men to her now scares them away. She'll never have a decent relationship until she deals with her real self—her inner fears and anxieties.

If you were writing her story, you'd probably want her to have a realization that she is more than her looks and start to believe in herself by the end. But this emotional transformation would have to happen throughout the story to show her in situations that would have her becoming emotionally stronger so that in the end her change and growth would be believable.

Characters are complex, just like you. They can experience extreme mood swings, from depression to happiness, from sorrow to joy, from love to hate. Your characters can be cautious, mistrusting, vulnerable, frightened, and adept at putting on a false front—smiling even though they're feeling fury, looking nonplussed when they're feeling emotional inside, acting sincere when they're lying.

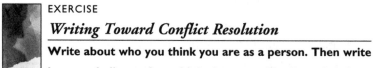

EXERCISE
Writing Toward Conflict Resolution

Write about who you think you are as a person. Then write how you believe others think about you. Finally, write about who you really are inside. How large is the gap between how others perceive you and the person you really are? How big is the gulf between who you think you are and who you really are? After you've answered these questions for yourself, do the same for your characters. How do your characters present themselves? What do your characters think about one another? Are your characters acting one way and feeling another? How? Do your characters ever show who they really are?

Let your characters resolve their conflicts in your stories through their behaviors and actions, and allow your readers and viewers to feel what your characters feel. ■ ■ ■

dysfunctional families: secrets, myths, and lies

> The greatest enemy of truth is very often not the lie—deliber-
> ate, contrived, and dishonest—but the myth—persistent, per-
> suasive, and unrealistic. —*John F. Kennedy*

*E*very family has a different way of interacting. Each has a different set of rules, values, myths, beliefs, secrets, traditions, lies,
and rituals. Some families are loud and verbal, others are quiet and
nonverbal, and still others are rigid and repressed. Some family styles
of operating are independent and individual; others are dependent
and enmeshed.

Dr. Murray Bowen of Georgetown University is the pioneer of
the family systems theory, which looks at the family as a system
rather than as separate individuals. His theory states that our family
units are the primary influences in our lives and that we are all
shaped by our respective family units. It is difficult for families to
change because their secrets, myths, and lies have been passed down
from generation to generation. By becoming familiar with your
character's family system and how he interacts with those in his
unit, you will be able to develop a deeper understanding of your
character's internal feelings, as well as with those who have influenced him. This knowledge will ultimately help you to create a
more realistic and complicated character.

151

Functional Families

The family is one of nature's masterpieces.

—*George Santayana*

Functional families have an open family system, which means the family is flexible, has open communication, is healthy, and has shared values and beliefs. In functional families, the individual members are less rigid, more supportive, and more loving with one another. They give positive rather than negative reinforcement in interactions with their children.

Parents of functional families show understanding and love to their children and accept them for who they are rather than forcing them to fit into a preconceived role of how a child should behave. Children from functional families have better self-esteem and confidence, develop friendships, and learn how to resolve conflicts in appropriate ways. Parents are good role models and able to express love to their children.

During the late 1950s and into the middle 1960s, television writers portrayed supposedly functional American families in shows such as *Father Knows Best, Leave It to Beaver,* and *My Three Sons.* These shows were unrealistically perfect versions of the all-American family.

While everyone aspired to create an idealized family, nobody succeeded because it was impossible. These perfect family portrayals wouldn't be as convincing to a modern audience because readers and viewers are too sophisticated to believe these types of families could ever exist. At one time or another, all families, even functional ones, have periods of crises and conflicts (however, they are not constant, like those of a dysfunctional family).

Dysfunctional Families

If you cannot get rid of the family skeleton, you may as well make it dance. —*George Bernard Shaw*

This chapter focuses on dysfunctional families and the traits that make them dysfunctional. A dysfunctional family has what is known as a closed system, where there is little freedom and greater parental con- trol. In order for you to create characters who are conflicted, confused, and complex, you need to understand the components of a dysfunctional family because problem-filled adults are the products of such families. In novels, films, and plays—such as Eugene O'Neill's *The Iceman Cometh,* John Updike's *Rabbit, Run,* and Norman Mailer's *An American Dream*—families are portrayed as having conflict between the parents, siblings, father and daughter, father and son, mother and daughter, or mother and son.

Every family lives with conflict. Even yours. You want to develop characters about families who go on a journey to succeed in overcoming their family problems. In some of the most powerful family dramas, the members never resolve their dilemmas, but the development comes from their taking the journey and their gradual recognition of their problems. It's important for you to learn some of the common traits of dysfunctional families, so when you create characters within a family unit, they'll be believable.

Traits in Dysfunctional Families

A man can't make a place for himself in the sun if he keeps taking refuge under the family tree. —*Helen Keller*

In a dysfunctional family, healthy functioning is impaired in such a way that it adversely affects every member of the family. Children of such families need to learn survival skills in order to withstand the family conflicts and dysfunction.

Dysfunctional families come in all shapes and sizes. They may be headed by two parents, or by parents who are divorced with a stepfather or stepmother taking the place of the birth father or mother. There are single parent families, joint custody families, blended families, same-sex families, and families headed by grandparents.

When you build a fictional family, use this information to realize all possibilities of families to create. Give your family of characters contrasting personalities so you have built-in conflicts and psychological problems. You want your families and your characters to be unique and yet, universal, so that everyone can identify and empathize with them.

Virginia Satir, a well-known marriage and family therapist and author of *Conjoint Family Therapy* and *Peoplemaking*, writes that the parents are the architects of the family. Parents who are emotionally disturbed create havoc in their families, leaving children feeling unprotected and insecure. When the parents in a dysfunctional family system have trouble coping and are overwhelmed because of their own immaturity, their children develop feelings of being unsafe.

In these family systems, if the parents aren't consistent and don't know how to parent, their children may experience an increased level of emotional turmoil and trauma. For example, a depressed parent may be emotionally unavailable to his or her children, and thus may seem distant or cold. This type of circumstance would naturally influence a child's emotional development.

Some families are too connected to their members. And other families become too detached from one another. Studies have shown that in both of these extremes, the families face problems that can be very hurtful to the children and can damage their self-esteem.

When you begin to create families, you don't have to build characters who are eccentric, weird, or outlandish. Just give your characters traits that appear in dysfunctional families and you will create characters who are filled with secrets, myths, and lies about themselves as well as their family or origin.

EXERCISE

Family Dynamics

What were the dynamics in your family? Describe in detail, writing with all of your five senses. What were some of the

major problems in your family? How were they solved? How did your family communicate with one another? Was your family open about its feelings? How did your parents show affection to each other? Were either of your parents depressed? How did you know?

Now think about your characters. What are the family dynamics of your characters? How do they communicate with one another in your story? How do your characters show affection towards one another? Does your character come from a depressed family? Is your main character depressed? ▪ ▪ ▪

Dysfunction Due to Death or Divorce

People living deeply have no fear of death. —*Anais Nin*

What happens to families when a death or a divorce occurs? In dysfunctional families, children can become traumatized by the disruption and feel rejected, insecure, and fearful. This is especially true in the case of divorce, in which one parent may play the other parent against the children by criticizing her ex or spoiling the children with lavish gifts. A parent also can sabotage the other parent by not being available when it's his day to have the children or by bringing them home later than they were supposed to return.

Children often blame themselves for the divorce in the family and have guilt that somehow they caused the divorce, perhaps by misbehaving and angering their parents. Many times this emotional fallout isn't considered by either parent, especially if one quickly remarries and has other children. Children of divorce can have a difficult time gaining back the security they had even in a dysfunctional family. It's of the utmost importance for the parents of these children to realize they have experienced a traumatic and stressful event and that they might need more care and even counseling to help them adjust.

It's imperative you learn what happens to people, and thus to your characters, during divorce or when there's a death in the family.

Characters become unbelievable when you don't know what their realistic emotional reactions should be. Grief often isolates members of the family from one another and can create chasms in families, ultimately tearing them apart.

An Edgar–award winning novelist who consulted with me on his latest novel created a character whose husband had just passed away. The character carried on as if nothing happened. This inaccurate portrayal of the way spouses really act at a time of death was completely unbelievable.

Since the death was an integral part of his main character's journey, the entire novel didn't work, and he had to rewrite it. After he learned the proper motivation for his characters in times of illness and death, he was able to successfully portray his characters' actions so they were believable.

As we learned in chapter one, psychiatrist Elisabeth Kübler-Ross's *On Death and Dying* looks at the five stages associated with death and dying: denial, anger, bargaining, depression, and acceptance. You need to become familiar with these stages so when you create characters going through a divorce or death, you'll be able to accurately portray their actions and reactions.

For example, let's suppose Fred, a married man for more than thirty years, discovers he has lung cancer. At first he is in denial, acts as if nothing happened, and continues to smoke. When he finally admits he's ill, he becomes angry, and when his wife and children try to talk to him, they have a difficult time communicating with him because he's so mad.

After he goes through denial and anger, he starts to bargain with God and with himself. He vows to his wife, "I swear I'll quit smoking if I can get better." He promises God that if he's cured, he'll donate his time to underprivileged children and the homeless.

After he realizes that he's not going to get better, he becomes depressed and can barely get out of bed. In fact, he refuses treatment to help him because he doesn't want to prolong his illness. He's given up.

Finally, he starts to accept the reality of his condition and decides   **157**
to live his remaining days to the utmost and to connect with his wife
and children to the best of his ability. He has gone through the five
stages of the grieving process and is now accepting his fate.

This example demonstrates how you can take your fictional characters
and make them believable when they grieve. You can motivate their
behavior when they are faced with an illness, divorce, death, or loss of
any kind.

These five stages can exist in other cases of loss, such as loss of a
job, loss of a child, loss of finances, loss of status, and loss of control
(being a victim of crime). There are also exceptions in the way people
grieve. Some stay stuck in the anger stage; others remain in denial
and don't face the reality of their grief.

The five stages may not always be so ordered. A person could enter
denial, become depressed, and then enter a denial stage again before
going on to bargaining. And the grieving process can go on for years,
sometimes never reaching a culmination. Characters can mourn a dead
child, husband, wife, or parents throughout your story. There are always
exceptions to the rules, and as long as you know the rules, you can break
them.

EXERCISE

Familial Influences

**Do you come from a divorced family? If so, which parent did
you live with? Is that the parent you wanted to be with? Was
your family a blended family or a nontraditional one? Are your parents
still married? If so, do you feel additional pressure to follow in your
parents' footsteps? When you hear people talk about their nontraditional families, how do their stories compare with yours?**

**Does your main character come from a divorced family? Which
parent does/did your character live with? Are any of your characters
separated or divorced? How do they cope with it?**

Take some of your characters and put them in a situation where they have to go through the five stages of grieving. Use your own emotions from your personal experiences to add a greater level of depth to your characters. Create a scene and let readers see them experience their actual feelings of grief. ■ ■ ■

Family Triangles

A person needs at intervals to separate from family and companions and go to new places. —*Katharine Butler Hathaway*

When you're having a problem with someone in your family, you may bring in a third family member to help reduce the anxiety and stabilize the relationship. This strategy is known as triangulating in another person to take your part and reduce your own stress. It's also somewhat of a coping method in that it offers an additional way for you to deal with and remedy difficult situations.

When a person calls in another family member to validate himself or reduce anxiety, it's often because he's unable to stand up for himself. The greater a family member's anxiety, the shorter the amount of time before he triangles in another member. Sometimes it's the parent, other times a sister or brother. It usually depends on who he believes will stand by him and take his part. The more rigid the roles in a family triangulation the more dysfunctional the family. This is especially true if a pattern develops where the same family members play the same roles in a triangle, and as a result, everyone in the family becomes limited in his or her reactions during conflict.

The roles in a dramatic triangle are persecutor, rescuer, and victim. The role each member of the family plays determines who's going to make up the family triangle. For example, if the mother always comes to her son's defense when he is berated by the father, then the triangulation is established: the mother is the rescuer, the father is the persecutor, and the son is the victim. The reverse is true when it's the father as the rescuer, mother as the persecutor, and daughter as the victim. Such patterns fall along Freud's theories of the Oedipus and Electra complexes. In the Oedipus Complex, which is based on the Myth of Oedipus in which Oedipus married his mother and killed his father, the son wants to marry his mother and kill his father. In the Electra Complex, the daughter wants to marry her father and kill her mother. By using such triangular relationships when developing your character and his family, you'll create fertile ground for interpersonal conflicts, heightened emotions and added tension.

You can see the dramatic triangle at work in Judith Guest's *Ordinary People*, which we discussed earlier. Conrad, the son, plays the victim; his mother, Beth, plays the persecutor; and his father, Cal, acts as Conrad's rescuer. The dramatic triangle creates conflict among the family members throughout the book. Even though Conrad isn't with his parents in this scene, as the subject of their argument, he is kept in the role of victim. Both parents are very familiar with the role they play as is evidenced in the following excerpt:

And, knowing that he [Cal] shouldn't, knowing somehow that it will only disarrange the contours of the day more thoroughly, still he says it: "I guess he didn't like the car."
. . . "I think," she says, "you worry too much about him."
"Yeah. And I think that you don't worry enough, but let it go, call it a very merry rugged Christmas Day, and let it go."
"And you expect too much. From all of us."

The argument continues and escalates:

"He's not your little boy," she says. "He'll be eighteen years old next month. For some reason, you want to think he needs your constant concern and protection. You worry over his every reaction. He smiles and you smile. He frowns and you baby him—"

"Okay, I'm concerned! Sometimes I worry! I'm *interested,* damn it! Are you interested?"

This argument illustrates the tension that can result from the dramatic triangle, as the marriage heads toward a major disaster.

It's important for you to know that a dramatic triangle isn't static and the family members can and do reverse their roles. A victim can become a persecutor, a rescuer can become a victim, and a persecutor can become a rescuer. That's what makes the dramatic triangle such an interesting element to use in your stories involving families.

EXERCISE
Characters in Triangular Relationships

What were the triangles in your family? How did they change between your parents and your siblings? What role did you play in the family triangulation and why? Do your characters have established roles in their families? Is your main character the rescuer, persecutor, or victim? Is the dramatic triangle in your character's family static or fluid? For example, does he go from victim to rescuer, or from persecutor to victim? ■ ■ ■

Family Secrets, Myths, and Lies

> No soul is desolate as long as there is a human being for whom it can feel trust and reverence. —*George Eliot*

There is a saying that goes, "You're as sick as your secrets." The same is true in the family system. Some families have more secrets than others. Healthy families try to be open in their communication and reveal secrets; dysfunctional families base so much of who they are on how they are looked upon by others that anything that would betray their outward image is kept secret. These families are filled with layer upon layer of secrets, and these secrets make them interesting characters for your stories.

When you create families for your stories you want them to have secrets that are revealed by the end of your story. Perhaps a family member has a dark secret, and everyone else in the family is invested in keeping it quiet. Creating characters and families with secrets gives you the opportunity to express their inner conflicts with their outward appearances. You've heard the expressions, "They have skeletons in their closet," and "They sweep everything under the rug." Well, it's true. In most families you will find that the family as a whole keeps secrets, or that individual family members do. By creating characters with secrets, you will have the chance to reveal their secrets, in the end, freeing them of the "ghosts of the past."

For example, let's say the mother of the family is having an affair with her brother-in-law, her husband's brother. In fact, the mother's youngest child resembles the uncle with her bright red hair. One of the children has discovered his mother and uncle kissing in a darkened hallway, but he quickly leaves, pretending nothing happened. He has never revealed his mother's secret and now he must keep it a secret, too. Maybe on some unconscious level, the husband and the rest of the children feel something is going on, but they ignore their inner whispers and intuition.

So all the members don't air their dirty laundry, and each goes on pretending all is well. This continues until the love affair fades, the mother asks for a divorce, or the husband finally confronts his wife and ends the marriage.

When you create characters with secrets, you must decide whether you want the secrets revealed, and, if you do, how you want to reveal them (directly or indirectly). If you have your characters reveal their secrets, you must also determine what the fallout will be. What price, if any, do your characters have to pay? Be sure to plan in advance not only what type of secret you'll give to your character, but also the outcome of having the secret revealed or kept in your story.

Dysfunctional families may have difficulty acknowledging their unpleasant truths, thus members have to pretend that everything is perfect all the time. For such dysfunctional families their concern is the outward impressions they give and how they behave in public. In my private practice, I work with many adults who are still grappling with whether or not they should reveal their family secrets. It's clear they feel discomfort when they eventually reveal secrets, even though they are now grown-ups. In fact, most act as though they are young children betraying family secrets. Just think about all the children who have been abused and keep their secret from teachers, school counselors, ministers, and doctors, never revealing that they've been assaulted. Even though they have visible bruises on their bodies, they will still lie to protect their parents.

When family secrets remain buried beneath the surface, the entire family presents a mask of the perfect family. A wonderful example of this dynamic occurs in the film *Far From Heaven.* Set in the 1950s, the family looks perfect but inside possesses dark secrets. The husband, a successful businessman, discovers he is gay and leaves his socialite wife for a man. She and her husband have to keep this secret from everyone at the risk of being ostracized by the friends in their social group.

Another destructive family secret found in real life may involve a child who begins to use drugs and starts to fail in school. When he's not hanging out with new friends, he stays locked in his room. His parents look the other way and avoid dealing with their son's increasing drug habit. Until something drastic happens (he steals money or jewelry, or becomes truant from school), the family will keep secrets and believe all the lies he tells them in order not to deal with the family problems beneath his drug use.

The same could be true for the alcoholic mother whose tendencies are kept secret by the children and husband. The father makes excuses that she is feeling sick when she can't get out of bed. He says that she's not an alcoholic and gets drunk after having only one drink.

An unhappily married couple may mask their problems by telling their children everything is fine, even though the father never comes home until after midnight because he is having an affair with another woman. The mother simply tells the children that he's working too hard in an effort to protect them from the painful reality.

It is necessary for families to lie to themselves so they don't have to deal with the dirt that they sweep under the rug. It's like playing a game of "let's pretend." The more secrets and lies a family keeps, the more dysfunctional the family becomes. A dysfunctional family is a family based on shoulds, oughts, have tos, and musts. If you're not entitled to feel what you're feeling and have to suppress those feelings, you soon become split from your feelings and become numb. You're constantly judged according to the rules of the family, who will go to any lengths to keep up their appearance of a happy family.

EXERCISE

Using Secrets and Lies to Reveal Conflict

What were some family secrets during your childhood? How were they kept or hidden away? What lies were you told to protect the family's image? What myths did your family pass down from generations? Write about the secrets and lies that were told in your family. Now describe the secrets that your character's family kept. What lies does your character's family tell to save face? Write a scene for each secret and lie, and let them be revealed in conflict between the family members. ▪ ▪ ▪

Alcoholism and Addiction

> Every form of addiction is bad, no matter whether the narcotic be alcohol or morphine or idealism. —*C. G. Jung*

Codependency is very prevalent in families of alcoholics and addicts. This is how it works: In a dysfunctional family, let's say the father is an alcoholic who comes home and drinks every night until he's drunk.

The mother tries to hide the fact from the children by making excuses for her husband. When he's too ill from a hangover to go to work, she calls his boss and lies, saying her husband is ill with the flu. The wife and husband are codependent upon each other. The husband drinks too much and his wife is an enabler. By making excuses to the children and lying to his boss, she enables him not to be responsible for his drinking and helps him hide the fact that he is an alcoholic.

In a family with an alcoholic or drug addict, codependency happens when one person is extremely dependent on the mate or parent. Some basic symptoms of codependency are having no boundaries, being too enmeshed with the significant other, and feelings that are fused with the other person. In most dysfunctional families, there is a great deal of codependency going on, but it is more prevalent in families of alcoholics and addicts.

Each parent can be codependent on the other, the children codependent on the parents, and the parents codependent on the children. In families and relations like this, the individual isn't able to recognize his or her own feelings as a separate person, and the environment is unsafe emotionally due to addictions, abuse and alcoholism.

Unfortunately, when a parent is an addict or alcoholic, he is in an altered state and indirectly is abandoning his children by not being available to them, even if he's home. Alcoholism and addictive behaviors in dysfunctional families can cause the children to feel emotionally abandoned, and they develop a tremendous craving for love.

Alcoholic parents are unpredictable and chaotic. They go from yelling and abusing their children one day to loving them and apologizing the next day. Children from alcoholic families become hypervigilant, taking their cues from their parents' moods, while at the same time ignoring their own feelings. In fact, some deny their own needs and wants just to placate their parents and make peace.

Many children in addicted or alcoholic families reverse roles with their parents and put them to bed when they're drunk or out of it.

They make the meals, clean the house, take care of the younger children, and tell lies to protect their parents. Of course, these children are on an emotional roller coaster. They're never permitted to be children. Abandonment is also a major issue in dysfunctional families. Parents abandon children through addictions by being emotionally unavailable, physically leaving them, not listening or hearing them, abusing them, or using them to help their marriage.

In some dysfunctional families, there is violence, especially if one parent is sober and the other isn't. The child has to keep the sober parent safe from the alcoholic one. Unfortunately, children from alcoholic families often become alcoholics and mirror their parents' behavior when they grow up.

With alcoholism or drug addiction, the focus of all the family from the spouse to the children is the addict. Everyone in the family fears the addicted member who often creates chaos in the family system. The rest of the family becomes aware of the addict's every move and walks on eggshells, hoping not to upset him or become victims of his rage.

You'll want to know how children survive when you create parents with problems of alcohol or drug abuse. If both parents are addicts or alcoholics, they may neglect their children and even endanger them. The children may also suffer emotional abuse should the parents scream or yell hateful and painful words at them while drunk. In order to accurately create fictional families of alcoholics or adult children of alcoholic parents, you want to familiarize yourself with the ways these families and individuals behave.

EXERCISE
The Role of Addiction in Fiction

Did your parents use alcohol or drugs? If the answer's yes, what did they do when in they were drunk or stoned? In what way were your parents or siblings codependent? How did

this affect the family? Did you trust your parents when they were using or did you not know what to expect from them? If the answer's no, think about stories you've heard from those who were raised by parents suffering from addictions. What emotions did they exhibit?

Do any of your characters come from families of alcoholics or addicts? If yes, what was the family system like? Who was codependent on the other and who was the enabler? Are any of your characters addicts or alcoholics? How do they behave to each other? How do any of your characters' addictions affect their relationships and family life? ■ ■ ■

Mental and Physical Abuse

> Collective fear stimulates herd instinct, and tends to produce ferocity toward those who are not regarded as members of the herd. —*Bertrand Russell*

Often parents who have been abused as children will be abusive to their own children and have no empathy for their children's emotional development. Their family life is filled with stress, chaos, disharmony, and frequently violence and substance abuse. Their children often become anxiety ridden and depressed because their parents are inconsistent in their behavior toward them. The parents are so unpredictable that the children always feel unsafe.

When you develop characters who've been abused, be sure to make them authentic by having them be filled with anxiety, depression, and low self-esteem. Don't tell the reader your characters are abused; show the results of their abuse through their behavior.

Abusive parents can abuse their children physically, emotionally, and sexually. Leaning more on a child than a spouse for solace and emotional connection is also a form of abuse because the child is being forced into an adult role. Parents who are absent due to work, illness, disability, or outside responsibilities also can create dysfunction in the family.

Making fun and being critical of a child is another form of abuse. The parents' own low self-esteem motivates them to take complete charge over their children and maintain power over even their minds.

In Tobias Wolff's *This Boy's Life,* the author describes the irrational and miserable existence heaped upon him by his stepfather, Dwight. Even though this book is a memoir, the techniques the author uses are applicable to the development of dysfunctional fictional characters. You, too, can use your childhood as fertile soil for your writing. Here is an excerpt of Wolff's first meeting with Dwight:

Dwight was a short man with curly brown hair and sad, restless brown eyes. He smelled of gasoline. . . . He dressed like no one I'd ever met before—two-tone shoes, hand-painted tie, monogrammed blazer with a monogrammed handkerchief in the breast pocket.

After his mother marries Dwight, Dwight changes into a brooding, angry man:

Dwight snarled so viciously that my mother felt obliged to put in a soothing word. He turned on her and said that as far as he knew he was still the father of this so-called family, or did she have another candidate?

"Dwight . . ." she said.

"Dwight," he mimicked, not sounding at all like her. . . . If my mother argued back he accused her of being disloyal, if she did not argue he became apoplectic with the sound of his own voice. Nothing could stop him but the sight of the Marblemount tavern.

Finally the emotional abuse becomes so bad that Wolff wants to run away:

> My idea was to steal enough to run away. I was ready to do anything to get clear of Dwight. I even thought of killing him, shooting him down some night while he was picking on my mother. . . . Sometimes I took the Winchester down when I heard Dwight start in on my mother, but his abuse was more boring than dangerous.

The above excerpts show the progressive level of tension existing within Wolff's family unit. Notice how the author illustrates his growing frustration and unhappiness through the way he chooses to describe Dwight—focusing on his outward appearance in the initial excerpt, on his hostile mannerisms and vocal criticisms in the second, and on his physical aggression in the third. These three excerpts combine to illustrate the effects of heightened tension and abuse on an individual's frame of mind.

Sexual abuse is often more subtle than fondling, inappropriate touching, or sexual intercourse. Seduction can be a form of sexual abuse, such as in the case of a parent who acts inappropriately with a child. Flirting or walking about naked when the child is too old is inappropriate and often confusing to the child of the opposite sex, especially when he or she gets sexual feelings. Letting the child sleep in the bed with the parents when he is obviously too old is another form of seductive behavior.

The most pervasive family secret is that of sexual abuse, usually perpetrated by a parent or relative. In most cases of incest, it's the fathers who sexually abuse their daughters. As I mentioned earlier, abused children often keep it a secret, fearing more harm will come to them and/or those they love should they reveal the truth.

In Dorothy Allison's *Bastard Out of Carolina*, Ruth Anne, the young daughter better known as Bone, has a new—and abusive— 169 stepfather. In the following excerpt, he is alone with her in a car:

Glen put his hand on my neck, and the stars seemed to wink at me. I wasn't used to him touching me, so I hugged my blanket and held still. He slid out from behind the steering wheel a little and pulled me up on his lap. He started humming to the music, shifting me a little on his thighs. I turned my face up to look into his eyes. There were only a few lights on in the parking lot, but the red and yellow dials on the radio shone on his face. He smiled, and for the first time I saw the smile in his eyes as plain as the one on his mouth. He pushed my skirt to the side and slid his left hand down between my legs, up against my cotton panties. He began to rock me then, between his stomach and his wrists, his finger fumbling at his britches.

It made me afraid, his big hand between my legs and his eyes glittering in the dim light.

This is the first time that Bone is a victim of her stepfather's sexual abuse, and she doesn't tell her mother about it, even though she is terrified of Glen. Notice how the author uses the detailed description to increase the level of tension within the passage. As the narrator, Bone's fear is clear from her description of the scene, making it easy for readers to empathize with her and share in her emotions.

Victims of abuse by a parent may not even tell their siblings or their other parent until they get the nerve to either confront the parent and make him stop, or until they leave home. In some families, the mother is unconsciously aware of what's going on but stays in denial, so she, too, is keeping the secret.

Discovery of the abuse usually comes from a school counselor, a family doctor, or an emergency room doctor, when a child is brought in for injuries inflicted by the parent. Sexual abuse transcends social status, economic position, education, religion, and race. There is permanent damage done to victims of sexual abuse that they need to work through in order to heal.

Although the responsibility for the abuse rests solely on the adult, survivors suffer feelings of shame, guilt, self-hate, low self-esteem, and insecurity. They are frequently self-destructive, and enter and stay in abusive relationships, or use drugs and alcohol to numb the pain. The most extreme result of sexual abuse is that when they're older, victims can and often do become abusers themselves.

EXERCISE
Creating Abused Characters

Did you suffer from any type of abuse in your family? How has it impacted your life? What feelings do you have concerning the abuse? Fear, shame, guilt, or blame? If you've never experienced any type of physical abuse, think about the stories you've seen on television, read in books, or even heard from friends. What type of emotions did those individuals exhibit? What was the long-term impact of this abuse?

Now, think about your characters. Is one of them a victim of abuse? If so, what type of abuse? Describe how the abuse has impacted your character? Now think about how the character's history of abuse could impact your overall story. ■ ■ ■

Family Rules and Beliefs

> Any fool can make a rule, and any fool will mind it.
> —*Henry David Thoreau*

Most families adopt traditions, rituals, perceptions, beliefs, values, and attitudes from their parents and grandparents. Family myths are evident in almost every family. Myths are stories we tell about ourselves to make sense of the world inside us and around us.

Many families have their own version of one of the following myths: We came over on the Mayflower. We are descendants from royalty. We Desmonds are from strong stock. Your grandfather was a wealthy landowner before everything was stolen from him. All the women in the Quinn family make great wives. Your great-grandfather was a highly decorated soldier in the Civil War.

These could be truths that have been passed down through the years and have become embellished, or they could be outright lies. There's the myth that the parents are really very happy, when in fact they're both miserable—this myth is created to protect the children. Yet, on some level everyone in the family knows it is false. There is the myth that the father is just too ill to work and can't get a job, when in fact he's too addicted to drugs to work and the mother is the breadwinner. These are just a few examples of family myths that help the family maintain whatever attitude they need to carry on about themselves.

In dysfunctional families, false beliefs are often the result of dysfunctional parents who blame their own children for their being sick or depressed. Children may be told, "You're making me sick," or "I work so hard for you and you don't appreciate anything I do." Children in such families suffer from shame and guilt for bringing unhappiness to their parents, even though they aren't the real cause.

Sibling rivalry can become a big problem in dysfunctional families, especially if the other siblings believe that their father favors a particular daughter or the mother has a special relationship with her older son. Parents who believe their mate has stronger affection for one of the children can be angry and blame the child for their marital problems. The child may then have the false belief that her parents' bad marriage is her fault and grows up with guilt.

When you want to breathe life into your characters, it will help if you decide in advance which family rules they adhere to. Be sure to give them beliefs that bring them in conflict with your other characters and that they learned from their family.

Other types of beliefs that are harmful in dysfunctional families are those that create biases and prejudices against people of other races, creeds, and religions. Political beliefs usually are passed down to the children. If the parents are conservative, the children will usually hold that political belief. If the parents are liberals, the children usually will follow suit. In fact prejudice, bias, and stereotyping are beliefs that are held by families for generations and are often passed down to children.

Some family rules are based on platitudes that have become integrated into the child's belief system, such as: "If you work hard, you'll be successful." "When the going gets tough, the tough get going." "It's not polite to brag about yourself." "Life is tough and then you die." "Men only want one thing." "You can't trust women." "You can only count on yourself." "Look out for number one." "It's not nice to think you're pretty."

EXERCISE

Writing Under the Influence of Traditions

What were some of the rules of your family when you grew up? Describe how they affect you now. What were some family beliefs? Do you still have the same beliefs today, and what is their impact on your life? What were some of the family rules for your characters? How do these rules affect your characters in your story? Do your characters still have the same prejudices and beliefs that the family had? Take some of your characters' beliefs and create a scene showing how these family beliefs can limit your characters' lives. ■ ■ ■

Family Injunctions

It is easier to pull down than to build up. —*Latin proverb*

In Eric Berne's best-selling book *What Do You Say After You Say Hello?*, he explains the principles of transactional analysis (which we looked at in chapter two) as "the study of ego states, which are coherent systems of thought and feeling manifested by corresponding patterns of behavior. Each human being exhibits three types of ego states which are The Parent, The Adult and The Child."

Your characters can behave from all three ego states in a story, just as individuals behave from these three ego states at different times in their lives. For example, if parents in a dysfunctional family are arguing, the wife might sound like a stern parent as she berates her husband: "I told you a hundred times to change your shirt before coming down to dinner." And he might respond from his child ego state: "Oh, I don't remember you telling me that." He's defending himself from criticism and blame just like a child does. These arguments go nowhere because they consist of blaming and defending oneself. Later, these roles may reverse, with the wife taking on the role of the child and the husband taking on the role of the parent.

In most dysfunctional families, the members operate from the child and parent ego state, and don't know how to relate in the adult to adult ego state, which doesn't include criticism, judgment, blame, and shame, but consists of mature people relating to one another in a direct manner. People who communicate from their adult ego state are reasonable and open to another person's ideas and thoughts without feeling defensive or threatened.

In transactional analysis there are what Berne calls injunctions, which are messages given by parents to a child that the child eventually integrates into his psyche. Injunctions that are given in childhood are carried throughout adulthood. The negative messages that you give to yourself originated in childhood with injunctions from your parents. These still remain with you in adulthood and develop into your inner critic. How you treat yourself as a grownup is probably how you were treated as a child.

Can you recall injunctions that your parents gave that you still carry with you now? Some of the messages in your childhood that

Berne refers to as injunctions could be: "Don't become a writer, get a real job." "You can't sing, why try?" "You're so lazy—you won't amount to anything." "You're too fat, why don't you try to lose some weight?" These injunctions can undermine your self-esteem and confidence all your life, unless you examine them and refuse to accept them.

When you begin to think about your characters for your story, it's important to develop and understand the injunctions each character was given in childhood. Decide when you're writing their backstory what injunctions they now believe. Their injunctions should justify what they believe about themselves presently in your story.

Maybe your female character believes she's unattractive because she was told by her mother and her father, "You're so awkward," "You're so clumsy," or "You should be modest." These injunctions would certainly create feelings of insecurity in your character.

EXERCISE
Critical Analysis

Growing up, what critical statements did you hear from your parents? What did they tell you about yourself? Write down at least five messages or injunctions that you received from each parent as a child. Are you still believing what they told you, and how does it affect your self-image now? Write down five messages or injunctions your characters were given in their childhood. Are they still affected by their injunctions, or have your characters overcome them? How do these messages affect your characters in their present? How can they give themselves new messages in your story? ■ ■ ■

Family Values and Traditions

Every man takes the limits of his own field of vision for the limits of the world. —*Arthur Schopenhauer*

Look at your family value system and traditions, and see how intertwined they are in your personality. If you have strong values and traditions, you can understand how you would get divorced if your spouse had radically different family values and traditions. Or maybe you'd quit a job because your value system was totally different from the way your boss operates his company. It's important for you to know and create your characters' family values and traditions in order to see the connection between them and their relationships in your story.

What a character would die for in a suspense novel or in a war story is clearly defined because there is a villain or an enemy who's obviously dangerous, so what your character would fight for and what he would die for are obvious.

Things are not as clear in romance novels and romantic comedies. When two characters first meet each other, you can create conflict by having your characters dislike each other because of their differing values and traditions. Yet, these two characters will eventually fall in love in spite of their different background and values.

Woody Allen demonstrates differences in values and traditions in *Annie Hall.* In it, he creates two disparate and humorous characters: Alvy Singer, a neurotic Jewish television writer from New York whose values and traditions are completely different from Annie Hall, a Protestant girl from the Midwest, who comes to New York to be a singer. She meets Alvy, and they fall in love. Her values, beliefs, and traditions are much different from his, and that's what sets up the comedy and the problems in the relationship.

You can see the extreme differences in their values and traditions in two simultaneous scenes that portray each family having dinner. In his family you see the family eating around a crowded dinner table, screaming, yelling, fighting, laughing, eating, and arguing all at once. In contrast you then see Annie Hall's family, in which they are very quiet, prim, and proper at the formal dinning table.

If you want to create a romantic relationship in your story, you can build characters who have different values, traditions, and beliefs from each other, because that is a way to create emotional conflict between them. As the characters recognize the futility of hanging on to old traditions and values, they will not only resolve their conflicts, but in the end transform themselves as well.

In my writing workshops, I always ask my students the following questions: "What would your characters fight for? What would your characters die for?" In every good novel or film you will discover that a character is fighting for something and would probably die for it if necessary. That is how you get meaning into your characters and give your story a plot that has purpose and a goal that is desperate.

However, you might be asking yourself, what about romance novels or romantic comedies? Maybe they wouldn't literally die in the same sense as in a war story or a crime novel, but maybe they would go to the ends of the earth for each other. A character's values and beliefs give meaning to your story. Family values, beliefs, and attitudes shape a child, and he usually adopts and keeps these values as a mature adult. Characters in your novel or film who come from different economic, social, and emotional backgrounds have different values, beliefs, traditions, and attitudes about life. These differences create sexual tensions and conflict between your characters.

What extraordinary measures would your characters take in their romantic relationships? Hopefully, by the end of your story, your romantic characters will both realize that they were lonely people and that they love each other and want to be a committed couple. You also want them to overcome their social, economic, and emotional differences by taking the journey together and being able to differentiate from their family.

EXERCISE
Imbuing Your Characters With Values

Write down all your own values, traditions, and rituals. What values were you taught in your family? Do you still have the

same values you grew up with? How have your values changed? What
were the three most important values in your family?
   Now, make a list of all your characters' values and traditions. How
do they enhance your characters' lives? Do any of your characters
change their values in your story? How? Are they influenced by another character? Do they have conflict with other characters because
of their values? What values would your characters die for? What
values would your characters fight for? ■ ■ ■

Dysfunctional Romantic Relationships

Love matches, so called, have illusion for their father and need
for their mother. —*Friedrich Wilhelm Nietzsche*

In love stories or romantic comedies, we usually read or see two people
falling madly in love, having problems within the relationship, and
finally having love conquer all. Writers are told boy meets girl, boy
loses girl, boy gets girl. And they both live happily ever after. We are
brought up with the belief that love conquers all and that when we
find the one we love, everything will be good and we'll be happy.
However, many of us wait for someone to save us from ourselves
because we hope to be rescued by the man or woman of our dreams.
A writer friend once quipped, "His neurosis met her neurosis across
a crowded room."

   Most of the time, each person in the relationship believes the other
will fulfill his or her hopes and dreams, and, ultimately, fill up the
emptiness each harbors inside. Since this is an impossible feat for
anyone to achieve, each eventually ends up disappointed and hurt by
the other because of unrealistic expectations.

   Men and women often fool each other, because they put on their
mask to make a great impression while inside they may be feeling
weak and frightened. So they fall in love with the false self of their
mate, each playing a role in order to make a great impression.

In relationships there are three entities: one individual, the other individual, and the relationship. In other words $1 + 1 = 3$. If the boyfriend has unresolved issues with his family and marries his girlfriend who still has issues from her family, the relationship will likely have many problems.

According to counselor John Bradshaw in his book *Bradshaw on: The Family*, dysfunctional families are created by dysfunctional relationships, which are created by dysfunctional individuals who marry each other. For example, a man who's unconsciously looking for a mother will marry a woman who he hopes will take care of him. When he's dating the woman, he acts sure of himself, and is confident and able to easily make decisions. At the same time, his girlfriend is looking for a good daddy to take care of her, and she expects her husband will protect and watch over her. While dating him she acts self-assured, makes dinners for him, and acts like a caretaker.

Both are behaving differently from the way they really are, hiding their own insecurities and low self-esteem. Their erroneous thinking is that their partner will take care of them, but the irony is that each partner has the same hope. Each is disappointed when the marriage doesn't work as planned.

In dysfunctional marriages, neither partner achieves real intimacy. The woman is disappointed that her husband doesn't live up to her expectations of him taking care of her, so she pulls away. Conversely, the husband has intimacy issues, so he's perfectly okay when his wife withdraws since he can't tolerate emotional closeness anyway.

When we fall in love, the excitement of marriage and raising a family together overtakes any notion that our marriage will end in divorce. Even though we hope our love will sustain and nurture us, 50 percent of married couples end up feeling disillusioned and get divorced. To develop characters who fall in love and are realistic, you need to give them problems to overcome, which will either make them closer or tear them apart. Though both individuals are disappointed in the relationship, they might remain together and have children, hoping that children will fill the emptiness in their marriage. This, of course, leads to a dysfunctional family, since the parents are the architects of the family and they aren't building a good foundation. Each spouse is dependent rather than independent or interdependent, and each continues to wait to be taken care of. When that doesn't happen, they each feel as if they've been duped, and the dysfunction persists if the couple remains together.

Children unconsciously mirror their parents, even though they swear they won't make the same mistakes their parents did, because that's how they've learned about relationships. They end up having self-defeating attitudes toward each other and being bitterly disappointed in not having their needs met.

EXERCISE

Romantic Disappointments

How are some of your characters disappointed in their mates? Are any of your characters in a conflicted relationship? If they are, describe their conflicted relationship. How do your characters behave before and after their marriage? Is there a big difference in who they are? Explain. ▪ ▪ ▪

Conflict in Dysfunctional Relationships and Families

All love that has not friendship for its base, is like a mansion built upon the sand. —*Ella Wheeler Wilcox*

Each person deals with conflict in different ways. Adults learn how to deal with conflicts in their childhood and continue coping with conflicts in their relationships and their eventual families. Children learn how to argue, shout, pout, and resolve conflicts from their parents. Some family members withdraw from conflict and put their heads in the sand. They may act as if nothing's wrong or escape by altering their mind through the use of drugs or alcohol. Other family members confront and face conflict immediately, often shouting, screaming, or yelling. The winner is the one who shouts the loudest. Others escape through having affairs instead of working through their problem.

In some families, the children and parents get over their anger immediately. In others, the family members hold grudges and resentments. Some families aren't allowed to express anger, and it instead expresses itself indirectly through passive aggressive or acting-out behavior. Then there are families who are into "gunnysacking," which is the act of storing up problems and allowing small irritations to build up until a person explodes in a rage because she didn't deal with the problems as they occurred.

Some couples come from argumentative families and others come from quiet families. Some deal with disagreements, while others avoid them. Some spouses confront conflict head on, while others do anything to deny or prevent it. When these disparate couples get together, they have different styles of dealing with conflicts. This, in turn, creates more conflicts because the couples are unable to find a common ground of conflict resolution.

EXERCISE

Communication and Conflict

How did your parents express their anger? What ways did your family resolve conflicts? What did your parents argue about? What was their most common argument? How were you allowed to express your anger? In your story, how do your characters express their anger? How do your characters resolve conflicts in their family? What methods do your characters use to express their anger indirectly? Are they successful dealing with their anger or are they afraid of it? ■ ■ ■

Homeostasis of the Family

Accept the things to which fate binds you, and love the people with whom fate brings you together, but do so with all your heart. —*Marcus Aurelius*

Change is difficult to achieve in a family system because patterns of behavior are passed down from generation to generation. Families maintain myths from the past, while simultaneously creating new ones to protect their homeostasis or balance. The family does everything possible to keep itself in balance, even if it becomes dysfunctional. A family is a system governed by its own rules and laws, which are instituted to keep the homeostasis in the family. When one member of the family gets out of balance another member will make up for the imbalance. In dysfunctional families, the rules are rigid and inflexible, while in healthy families the rules are flexible and negotiable.

The various types of emotional and psychological relationships we deal with in stories involve: dysfunctional families, sibling rivalries, father-son relationships, mother-daughter relationships, addictions, codependence, enablers, family system triangles, cultural differences, and family dynamics. These all affect the homeostasis of the balance.

In the beginning of any good story, the homeostasis or status quo of the characters is set off balance, which creates emotional conflict for all the characters, but most especially for the main character in your story. The characters' journey throughout your story is to achieve a new balance. By the end of the story, the characters are hopefully in a new state of homeostasis due to change and transformation. For example, in Alice Sebold's *The Lovely Bones*, the Salmon family is sent into a tailspin at the loss of their eldest daughter, Susie. The novel charts the family's descent into grief, blame, and fragmentation, but in the end, the family emerges intact, having found a new balance.

Establishing Homeostasis

What do your characters do to keep their homeostasis? At the beginning of your story, what crisis or problem have you set up to threaten the homeostasis? What actions do your characters take to get back their homeostasis or create a new balance? By the end of your story, do your characters have a different homeostasis, and is it for the better or for the worse? ■ ■ ■

Finding Your Character's True Self

As a man thinketh in his heart, so is he. —*Proverbs 23:7*

As children, we often blamed ourselves for the problems in our dysfunctional family. Eventually we must recognize that we can't change anyone else, only ourselves. The same is true for your fictional characters. You need to allow your characters to take the first small step of trusting to let others know who they are.

In *Ordinary People*, Conrad is suspicious and doubtful about his psychiatrist, Dr. Berger, until little by little he begins to trust him, and, in turn, begins to trust himself. Conrad is able to reveal his inner feelings: his anger, disappointment, and guilt about his brother's death. As he lets go of his painful feelings and tells them to another person, he starts to heal his personal pain, which originated in his family. Through therapy, he learns how to accept himself and about his ability to care and to love, even though his mother will never love him the way he desires. He experiences an emotional transformational arc and gains an inner confidence and a new independence from his parents, especially his mother.

When you create characters from dysfunctional families and relationships, help them overcome their childhood pain, blame, hurt, and shame by having them focus on themselves. Your characters are bound to repeat the past unless they can observe themselves, their beliefs, and values. You want your characters to regain their true selves.

Your writing goal is to build characters who are capable of dealing with their own actions and reactions. You need to motivate your characters so they will cast off their dysfunctional family secrets, myths, and lies. Most of all, you want to create characters who are able to change the limited beliefs and rigid rules inherited from their family into unlimited opportunities for personal growth, insight, and transformation.

creating real people: disorders and troubled personalities

The proper study of mankind is man. *—Alexander Pope*

*P*eople love to read about characters who are different from them. They enjoy being entertained by characters who are deviant, difficult, and diverse. To catch the attention of these readers, you must become familiar with different types of personality disorders to create characters who will be psychologically real. In this chapter, you'll learn how to create a tableau of interesting characters—from neurotics to psychotics.

To create complex characters, it is necessary for you to have more knowledge about emotionally troubled individuals and mental illness. It's not enough to create a detective who solves a crime. It's important to have psychologically troubled individuals commit these crimes. Well-known mystery writers, such as Jonathan Kellerman, a former child psychologist, write about sociopaths and psychopaths because readers are intrigued with these characters. The detective in a psychological novel works on two levels. He not only wants to discover who the perpetrator of the crime is but also what makes him tick. The "why" of the criminal takes equal if not more precedence over who has committed the crime.

In the novel *Misery* by Stephen King, the character Annie Wilkes is a troubled personality. In the book, a novelist, Paul Sheldon, is in a car accident and breaks his leg and arm. Annie rescues him and takes him to her house to recuperate, but it turns out she wants more than to help him. She wants him to resurrect Misery, the fictional character he'd killed off in his last novel.

On the outside Annie is smiling and nurturing; in reality, she is sedating him and he becomes a prisoner in her home. As the story unfolds, the reader realizes Annie is a complete psychopath. Annie's troubled personality and her unpredictable behavior combine to make the novel successful. Her deviant behavior and warped thinking are shocking and terrifying, and readers breathlessly want to know what's going to happen next. Stephen King portrays her in such a way that she draws readers in with her seemingly nice smile and her caretaking. Yet, she's a time bomb waiting to explode (just like another of his successful characters, Carrie, in the novel of the same name).

Understanding Troubled Personalities

It is noteworthy that persons are pronounced mad by officials destitute of evidence that they themselves are sane.

—Ambrose Bierce

Today's readers want to be amazed and suspended in wonderment. They want to understand the motivations of troubled personalities and comprehend how they got to be that way. If you want to be at your creative best, build psychologically deeper characters and emotionally complex personalities for your fiction and films. When you accomplish this goal your readers and viewers will be involved in your stories and root for the hero and against the villain.

All stories deal with the characters' problems, conflicts and troubles, which hopefully are solved and resolved in the end. It is the troubled, twisted or tormented characters that capture your readers' and viewers' imagination and create excitement in your stories. In order for you to write about such characters, you need to delve into their minds to understand their psychology. As you begin to study the nature of personality and emotional states, you'll create complex characters who are disturbed in a realistic and believable manner.

You may wonder why it's necessary for you to learn about individuals who are neurotic or psychotic. In order to be a contemporary writer, you'll want to learn certain traits and characteristics of troubled personalities so that you can realistically portray their dementia and delusions, their psychoses and neuroses.

You don't have to be a psychologist to understand characters who are different, but you do need to be familiar with and aware of individuals whose personalities are warped or wicked, mad or menacing, phobic or psychotic. It's not only important, but a must for you to become familiar with the most common types of personality disorders as portrayed in popular novels or films.

Many wonderful stories can also be ruined if the writers don't bother to take the time to research how characters react to real problems. Many writers may not know what happens to a person if she's raped or how characters behave if they're victims of abuse. These behaviors and reactions are of the utmost importance for you to become familiar with; otherwise, your characters won't be believable and your stories will fail. If someone reading your story or watching your film knows the reality of how a person behaves in such painful circumstances and your portrayal isn't accurate, your characters won't ring true and you risk losing your reader's interest.

Recently, I consulted with a professional writer who had written several published novels. In his latest work, he wrote about a woman who was raped. I was incredulous when I read that the woman was joking and laughing with her friends, including the man who raped her, the next day. Yes, she knew him, and yes, they were on vacation on a boat with a group of other friends, but she went through a traumatic experience. The entire story seemed false after that incident because the characters behaved in an unrealistic way. The writer hadn't researched the reactions of rape victims or why someone becomes a rapist.

Your fictional situations have to be authentic, and you should be familiar with the reactions people have to death, divorce, betrayal, incest, rape, and illness. Although these aren't categorized as personality disorders, they are subjects that frequently are written about in novels and films. By having a basic understanding of certain types of personality disorders and life situations that your characters will encounter, you will be able to create characters with realistic behaviors.

The Human Condition and Troubled Personalities

I know the purity of pure despair, / My shadow pinned against a sweating wall. —*Theodore Roethke*

At some time in their lives, many individuals suffer from some type of emotional disturbance, such as a bout of depression, an anxiety attack, or a bad case of nerves. Just to be alive in today's world is to be vulnerable to emotional distress and the personal stress of daily living. Your fictional characters should reflect what is happening in your society and in your culture. It's all part of being human, part of the human condition. These feelings eventually pass and life goes on, but when troubled personalities suffer from such disturbances, these conditions don't go away but become more intense. Their emotional disturbances often become chronic and these individuals are considered disturbed personalities.

When you deal with these conflicts, they should emanate from the character's personality. Aside from the action in a story, the more important conflict is that between characters in a relationship or within the character himself. In fact, the most powerful stories deal with some type of internal discord within a character, which usually begins with fear of a particular situation, person, or circumstance.

There are a multitude of categories for individual psychological problems and pathology. However, this is not a chapter on psychology but a chapter on showing you how to write about the different types of emotional and psychological disturbances which your characters might experience.

As a psychotherapist, I consult with clients and make an assessment regarding their diagnosis according to the established manual used by all therapists, known as the *Diagnostic and Statistical Manual of Mental Disorders* or DSM-IV. You'll be able to refer to DSM categories in this chapter for information on portraying fictional characters with mental disorders. It's important to note that a character can sustain various traits from different categories. These are just psychological guidelines to use when creating characters; they aren't written in black and white but are painted in shades of gray, just like memorable characters.

Neurotics: The Common Variety of Real People

Everything we think of as great has come to us from neurotics. It is they and they alone who found religions and create great works of art. —*Marcel Proust*

The neurotic personality hasn't broken with reality but is an individual, just like you and me, who is at odds with her life. She's often perceived as trying to make the best of things in a miserable world. The neurotic frequently has a lot of anxiety, restlessness, depression, inner conflicts, fears, doubts, and tension, but is still able to function. Neurotics are very prevalent; we all struggle with life problems. Problems of adjustment such as fear of being liked, fear of being rejected, fear of being hurt, and even fear of success are universal.

When you create characters who are neurotic, you must be able to lay down their motivation and make their behavior realistic. You need to make them consistent in personality so they'll be believable. You must build their backstory by understanding their childhood.

Neurosis is considered a functional disorder that often involves the thwarting of a character's fundamental urge. It's an inner struggle that individuals suffer. Neurotics operate within reality and can function within society's norms and rules, yet their anxiety, worry, or physical symptoms may cause distress in social or work-related situations, along with other areas of functioning.

Other well-known symptoms from neurosis are impatience, irritability, hypersensitivity, and worry. It becomes difficult for individuals to control the worry and to cope with daily problems. They become easily fatigued and have difficulty concentrating. Some neurotics have muscle tension and experience sleep disturbances.

Many neurotics are hypochondriacs. Hypochondria is a neurosis that manifests itself by an individual's preoccupation with physical ailments. These ailments are sometimes real but mostly imagined. When the person has real physical symptoms, there is often no discernible organic cause. However, the fear of illness continues and often leads to the fear or belief of having a serious illness, even though there is no evidence.

A great example of neurotic personalities can be found in the characters portrayed by writer/director Woody Allen. In *Hannah and Her Sisters*, Woody plays the role of a neurotic character, Mickey, who is the writer of a television show. He is always worried about getting ill and fears he is going to die of a brain tumor after he fails a hearing test. The audience can identify with him, recalling their own fears of imagining a serious illness when going to the doctor for a simple test. This character connects to others and that's why he was such a successful character.

The portrayal of the character's neurosis can come from your own fears, anxieties, doubts, and worries. Use yourself and your childhood memories as resources for your troubled characters and you will breathe life into them.

Often people become neurotic because of overbearing and critical parents who try to run their children's lives, even when they're adults. A good example of such a parent can be found in the mother in Helen Fielding's *Bridget Jones's Diary*. Let's take a look at another excerpt from that book:

> My mother rang up at 8:30 in the morning last August Bank Holiday and forced me to promise to go. She approached it via a cunningly circuitous route.
>
> "Oh, hello, darling. I was just ringing to see what you wanted for Christmas."
>
> *"Christmas?"*
>
> "Would you like a surprise, darling?"
>
> "No!" I bellowed. "Sorry. I mean . . ."
>
> "I wondered if you'd like a set of wheels for your suitcase."
>
> "But I haven't got a suitcase."
>
> "Why don't I get you a little suitcase *with wheels attached.* You know, like air hostesses have."
>
> "I've already got a bag."
>
> "Oh, darling, you can't go around with that tatty green canvas thing. You look like some sort of Mary Poppins person who's fallen on hard times. Just a little compact case with a pull-out handle. It's amazing how much you can get in. Do you want it in navy on red or red on navy?"
>
> "Mum. It's eight-thirty in the morning. It's summer. It's very hot. I don't want an air-hostess bag."

It is all too obvious that Bridget's mother is indirectly criticizing her daughter, while simultaneously trying to control her. Is it any wonder that Bridget is neurotic?

Emotional Problems

Emotional difficulties in neurotics are often the result of their inability to deal with life problems in an effective manner because of never having learned how to cope with childhood experiences. Childhood neuroses can begin when children are raised with constant abuse and deprivation, or in a home with constant arguing. They won't feel safe, and often become self-destructive adults filled with low self-esteem.

If you wonder how to develop a neurotic character for your story, look around you for models and you'll find them everywhere you go—in your family, at work, with friends, school, and church. We all have some neurotic tendencies, which are either obvious or secretly kept hidden away.

Your fictional characters are filled with fear of the dark, fear of failure, fear of intimacy, fear of rejection, fear of abandonment, and many other types, which are hidden away in the closet of the self. They are reined in until, under pressure, some clues, such as low self-esteem, nerves, anxiety, or a bad reaction to life's daily stress, begin to leak out.

Social Readjustment Rating Scale

Adults who suffer from neurosis often experience it in middle age because of a trauma in their lives. It could be caused by a death in the family, illness, disability, divorce, losing one's job, overcoming illness, getting in debt, an empty nest, moving, or losing one's social status. These stressful situations can provoke an onset of emotional or neurotic problems.

The Social Readjustment Rating Scale (SRRS), which was developed by Thomas H. Holmes and Richard H. Rabe and appeared in the *Journal of Psychosomatic Research* in 1967, measures the magnitude of stressful situations that individuals experience in their life. Although it doesn't include many types of stressful situations, it does deal with the readjustment that these stressors require. I'm including the first ten so you can become familiar with what situations your characters could have which might bring out their neurotic symptoms. Each life event has a Life Change Unit that is a value that is rated to the event. The more stressful the life event the higher the Life Change Unit Value.

SOCIAL READJUSTMENT RATING SCALE

Life Event	*Life Change Unit Value*
1. Death of a spouse	100
2. Divorce	73
3. Marital separation	65
4. Jail term	63
5. Death of a family member	63
6. Illness or injury	53
7. Marriage	50
8. Fired from job	47
9. Marital reconciliation	45
10. Retirement	45

These ratings are arbitrary but give you a sense of how stressed your characters will become in these specific life situations. The SRRS is an excellent way for you to realize the relationship between your character's situation and her need for adjustment. Although most of these situations are negative and certainly would motivate your characters to be in a crisis state, positive events, like getting a job promotion, falling in love, moving to a new house, and graduating from college or law school, are also stress-provoking.

By referring to the top ten stressors in the SRRS, you can immediately create conflict, stress, and tension within your characters. By putting your characters into some of the above situations, you'll have built-in conflicts that make for dramatic stories and might even cause your characters to become neurotic. For example, in Louis Begley's *About Schmidt*, the story picks up just after the main character's wife dies. The ramifications of her death are visible in his thoughts and behavior throughout the novel.

Neurotics also have feelings of low self-esteem, little self-worth, and inferiority. An extreme neurosis interferes with one's ability to function in daily life or in relationships. However, the everyday neurotic personality is able to live in the world and conform to the rules of society. In fact, neurotics operate at a high level, in spite of what disturbances they feel, even in the grips of their neurotic symptoms.

I want go out on a limb here: I believe that most stories that show any depth of character deal with some type of neurotic trait such as depression, insecurity, fear, self-doubt, or anxiety. Just think of all the classic characters in literature, and you'll discover that this is true. Immortal characters such as Hamlet, Heathcliff, King Lear, Othello, Willie Loman, Mrs. Dalloway, Laura Wingfield, Lolita, and Jane Eyre all had interpersonal neurotic problems, and some even became psychotic.

EXERCISE
Characters, Stress, and Conflict

Write a scene in which a character experiences a highly stressful event. How does your character deal with the stress? Write about the conflict your character faces by just experiencing one of the SRRS's top five stressors. Describe how your character behaves when dealing with the stress.

Certain behaviors give clues that an individual might have emotional problems. Some of the most common behaviors are excessive moodiness, constant worry, ruminating, sudden mistrust of others, suspiciousness, unreasonable belligerence towards others, hypochondria, and spending more time in fantasy than in reality. To have these behaviors doesn't imply emotional illness, but continual frequency of such problems means the person needs professional treatment. Neurotics also develop many defense mechanisms against anxiety. The background of troubled people plays an important role in their emotional life. ■ ■ ■

Personality Disorders

We are all born mad. Some remain so. —*Samuel Beckett*

Personality disorders are usually characterized by the presence of maladaptive patterns of behavior and perception that impact the individual's emotional and social functioning. Personality disorders aren't illnesses. They're deeply ingrained erroneous ways of thinking, behaving, and feeling that impair a person's functioning or cause him emotional distress. Personality disorders are often shaped by a person's upbringing and childhood experiences.

Individuals who develop personality disorders often have poor functioning skills, trouble with the law, no work, no friends, and no social skills. Many have had problems in relationships with other people and their family. Individuals who suffer from personality disorders display abnormal behavior, which creates a chaotic life filled with disruption in their thinking, moods, and impulse control.

Susanna Kaysen, the author of *Girl, Interrupted* ends up in a mental institution after trying to commit suicide. She tells the story about her time spent in the hospital and of the other patients who she befriends. She describes her diagnosis of personality disorder as follows:

> Sometimes they called it a personality disorder. When I got my diagnosis it didn't sound serious, but after a while it sounded more ominous than other people's. I imagined my character as a plate or shirt that had been manufactured incorrectly and was therefore useless.

If you're going to create a character with a personality disorder, it's important for you to be familiar with various characteristics of specific disorders. Even if your character is unsure of what her disorder means, it's important for you, as the author, to make it clear for readers. Otherwise, readers will have a difficult time connecting on an emotional level with your character.

To give you an idea of some of the basic traits that best reveal a character's type of disorder, let's look at some of the most dominant personality disorders seen in fiction:

Histrionic Personality Disorder

Individuals with this disorder, which is more common in women, often exhibit intense, dramatic behavior, crave excitement, and are highly reactive and excitable. They have tendencies toward being dependent on another person, and toward exaggerated displays of emotional reactions and sudden emotional changes. A good example of a character who has a histrionic personality disorder is Blanche DuBois, the main character in Tennessee Williams's play, *A Streetcar Named Desire*, which we discussed earlier in chapter two. Blanche vacillates between arrogance when she looks down at her lower class brother-in-law, Stanley, to being desperate as she tries to seduce Mitch, a friend and co-worker of Stanley's. Throughout the play she drifts off into fantasies and memories of her past, including the suicide of her homosexual young husband. She finally goes over the edge from hysteria to psychosis and is taken away to a mental institution. Blanche is one of the most complex and famous female characters in literature.

Borderline Personality Disorder

Individuals with this disorder may exhibit impulsive behavior and find it difficult to establish interpersonal relationships. Individuals with this disorder are often intense in relationships and alternate between idealizing or castigating the other person. The character of Virginia Woolf in Edward Albee's play *Who's Afraid of Virginia Woolf* exemplifies a borderline personality. One moment she's cruel to her husband, George, and the next minute she's kind. She becomes overly-emotional when drunk, and is abusive to him. Her feelings of emptiness are chronic and her behavior is reckless.

Borderlines participate in such self-destructive behaviors as speeding, binge eating, or substance abuse. Fears of abandonment and feelings of inappropriate anger bring about constant arguing with others, sometimes to the point of physical violence. The individual experiences distorted thoughts and perceptions, particularly in interpersonal relationships. Many borderline personalities come from dysfunctional families with a background of emotional, physical, or sexual abuse.

Narcissistic Personality Disorder

Individuals with this disorder have a false sense of self-importance, crave power, and are self-centered. They suffer feelings of grandiosity and like to be admired. They also lack empathy toward other people and are insensitive to others' feelings. At the same time, they are extremely hypersensitive. They often have inflated opinions of themselves and are arrogant and pompous toward others. In addition, they often surround themselves with people who will bolster their sense of self-worth and who will appreciate and admire them.

In Oscar Wilde's *The Picture of Dorian Gray,* Dorian is a great example of a narcissistic personality. He wants eternal youth and fantasizes that he'll never grow old. The following shows Dorian's reaction upon first seeing the portrait of himself:

> When [Dorian] saw it he drew back, and his cheeks flushed for a moment with pleasure. A look of joy came into his eyes, as if he had recognized himself for the first time. He stood there motionless and in wonder, dimly conscious that Hallward was speaking to him, but not catching the meaning of the words. The sense of his own beauty came on him, like a revelation. . . . Yes, there would be a day when his face would be wrinkled and wizen, his eyes dim and colourless, the grace of his figure broken

and deformed. The scarlet would pass away from his lips and the gold steal from his hair. The life that was to make his soul would mar his body. He would become dreadful, hideous and uncouth.

As he thought of it, a sharp pang of pain struck through him like a knife and made each delicate fibre of his nature quiver. His eyes deepened into amethyst, and across them came a mist of tears. He felt as if a hand of ice had been laid upon this heart.

Like the Narcissus of mythology, Dorian is completely in love and enthralled with his own beauty. The mere thought that his beauty may one day fade brings tears to his eyes. For Dorian, everything revolves around him and his beauty, and the author reinforces this sentiment through word choice and description.

Obsessive-Compulsive Disorder

A person suffering from Obsessive-Compulsive Disorder (OCD) often has irrational thoughts or feelings. These thoughts persistently intrude into one's consciousness and can't be stopped, resulting in repetitive and uncontrollable compulsions. Compulsions are irrational acts a person can't stop doing, like jumping over cracks in the sidewalk, throat clearing, hand washing, and repeatedly stopping the car to check if it's been hit by another car. These acts can make life miserable for an individual and prevent him from living a normal life. Sufferers are typically inflexible perfectionists who are overly conscientious and often depressed and anxious.

In *The Matchstick Men*, a novel by Eric Garcia, the con artist, Roy, is an example of a functioning character with OCD. During the story, Roy runs out of his medicine. He becomes cautious, and, without his medicine, his disorder takes over. He begins to hoard his money inside a ceramic horse, has difficulty leaving the house, and feels sick at the sight of dirt—all of which add levels not only to the character of Roy, but also to the entire story.

Garcia has created a character who demonstrates the compulsions of and the frustration in having OCD. By giving Roy a personality disorder, he has added a wealth of dimension to his con-artist character.

Paranoid Personality Disorder

A paranoid personality is a person who has a distrust of others. Paranoid Personality Disorder is an emotional disorder causing excessive worry without any specific cause. Children with it become excessively dependent on their parents and fearful and timid with others, especially their peers. They have an unreasonable belief that others are trying to harm or deceive them. Adults with it are guarded, secretive, frightened, and harbor a pervasive mistrust. Suspicious of other people, they imagine threats and conspiracies by others, including spouses. They often suspect their spouses of infidelity, hold grudges, and constantly perceive danger in their environments. Many villains in books and films are paranoid personalities.

People who become addicted to drugs or alcohol also may exhibit paranoid tendencies, especially those who are heavy users of cocaine. As the addiction increases, the addict starts to exhibit paranoia and irrational thinking. I've dealt with a client who used cocaine, and, experiencing a temporary bout of paranoia, hid in the closet all day, imagining that someone was in the house and going to kill her.

Alcoholics who are out of control and spiraling downward often suffer from delirium tremors, an extreme manifestation of paranoia. They become irrational and imagine all types of horrific situations, such as spiders crawling all over them.

Dissociative Identity Disorder

Dissociative Identity Disorder is also referred to as Multiple Personality Disorder. This disorder is usually caused by some type of painful emotional crisis from which one wishes to escape; sufferers detach and dissociate from the pain, thus escaping conscious contact from reality. Dissociative Identity Disorder can be caused by some traumatic childhood situation such as sexual or physical abuse. Usually, as a result of the crisis and the need to escape pain, two or more identities control the person's behavior at different times. These various identities are referred to as alters and exhibit different personalities and physical appearances. Symptoms also include depression, anxiety, conduct problems, hallucinations, and difficulty in interpersonal relationships.

Dr. Jekyll and Mr. Hyde by Robert Louis Stevenson features a character with a multiple personality. Dr. Jekyll is a good, kind doctor who turns into the evil Mr. Hyde by means of a potion he created in an experiment. He vacillates between the two personalities and can't remember what he did as the evil Mr. Hyde. Dr. Jekyll realizes that Mr. Hyde commits crimes and has even murdered people, and he decides not to drink the potion anymore to remedy the evil. However, Mr. Hyde has become an irrevocable part of Dr. Jekyll, and Jekyll can't stop him from taking over his personality. In the following excerpt, you'll see how Dr. Jekyll acknowledges—and tries to make sense of—his own duality:

> With every day, and from both sides of my intelligence, the moral and the intellectual, I thus drew steadily nearer to that truth, by whose partial discovery I have been doomed to such a dreadful shipwreck: that man is not truly one, but truly two. I say two, because the state of my own knowledge does not pass beyond that point. Others will follow, others will outstrip me on the same lines; and I hazard the guess that man will be ultimately known for a mere polity of multifarious, incongruous, and independent denizens. I, for my part, from the nature of my life, advanced infallibly in one direction and in one direction only. It was on the moral side, and in my own person, that I learned to recognise the thorough and primitive duality of man; I saw that, of the two natures that con-

tended in the field of my consciousness, even if I could rightly be said to be either, it was only because I was radically both; and from an early date, even before the course of my scientific discoveries had begun to suggest the most naked possibility of such a miracle, I had learned to dwell with pleasure, as a beloved day-dream, on the thought of the separation of these elements. If each, I told myself, could but be housed in separate identities, life would be relieved of all that was unbearable; the unjust delivered from the aspirations might go his way, and remorse of his more upright twin; and the just could walk steadfastly and securely on his upward path, doing the good things in which he found his pleasure, and no longer exposed to disgrace and penitence by the hands of this extraneous evil. It was the curse of mankind that these incongruous fagots were thus bound together that in the agonised womb of consciousness, these polar twins should be continuously struggling. How, then, were they dissociated?

Phobias

I suppose our capacity for self-delusion is boundless.
—*John Steinbeck*

The Phobic Reaction has different types: specific phobias and social phobias. Specific phobias cause people to have irrational fears about something that in actuality poses no danger to them. The irrational fear leads to avoidance of situations and causes the individual to have a limited life. Social phobia is fear of other people, of being humiliated, embarrassed, or judged. It leads to an irrational dread of an object, situation, or person. A basic fear or feelings of insecurity often are displaced or put onto a specific phobia.

One type of phobia is agoraphobia, a fear of open places, which prevents a person from going out. When she does go out, she becomes so frightened, she can experience a panic attack. Many agoraphobics fear crowds, shopping malls, restaurants, riding on buses, subways, and leaving home. Some individuals restrict their world to what they consider a safety zone, often their home and sometimes an area immediately surrounding it. Many people are entirely disabled by their condition and unable to work, shop, or leave their home.

Acrophobia is a fear of high places. An example of a character having acrophobia can be found in Alfred Hitchcock's film *Vertigo*, in which the character Scottie, a San Francisco police detective, is afraid of heights because he almost fell to his death from a rooftop. His character also feels guilty because a fellow officer and friend died trying to rescue him. Scottie's phobia of heights immobilizes him and plays into his character.

EXERCISE

What's Ailing Your Character?

Use the above descriptions of various disorders and phobias to create a character with each of the following:

1. **Create a character who has Obsessive Compulsive Disorder, and reveal how the disorder manifests itself during the scene.**

2. **Create a character who demonstrates some type of phobia, and show how it hinders his behavior.**

3. **Create a character who has a Narcissistic Personality Disorder, and have her be in conflict because of her narcissism.** ■ ■ ■

Anxiety Disorders

> The feeling of being disintegrated, of being unable to experience emotions, of losing one's objects, is in fact the equivalent of anxiety. —*Melanie Klein*

The Anxiety Reaction involves having feelings of apprehension and anxiety without a specific reason or cause. It is often referred to as "free-floating anxiety." Individuals experience heart palpitations, shortness of breath, sweating, and tremors, which cause them great distress. These are in reaction to an unconsciously imagined threat to one's goals or status. Accompanying these symptoms are feelings of insecurity and low self-esteem. Anxiety is an unpleasant state of tension, but unlike fear, which occurs due to a specific event, person or situation, anxiety keeps one in a jumpy, nervous state, without any particular stimulus.

Generalized Anxiety Disorder

This is a chronic, often debilitating condition that consists of excessive worry, tension, and jumpiness. It causes restlessness, sleeplessness, irritability, lack of concentration, fatigue, hyper-vigilance, and heart palpitations. Post-Traumatic Stress Disorder (PTSD) and Panic Disorder are different types of Anxiety Disorders.

Post-Traumatic Stress Disorder

PTSD is a delayed reaction that occurs after experiencing or being a witness to a traumatic situation or event, such as a criminal assault, sexual abuse, war, terror, rape or a disaster of nature such as an earthquake or tornado. People suffering from PTSD have flashbacks, nightmares, and depression. They often can't hold a job and turn to alcohol or drugs to numb their feelings of panic. In women, the most common precipitating events for PTSD are rape and physical assault. For men, seeing someone seriously hurt or killed and physical assault are the most prevalent.

In Judith Guest's *Ordinary People*, which we discussed earlier, Conrad Jarrett suffers from PTSD after his brother drowns in a boating accident trying to save him. He experiences flashbacks and night sweats, and even attempts suicide.

Panic Disorder

Panic disorder occurs after a person suffers from undue stress or anxiety, and often runs in families. People may feel like they're having a
heart attack because the symptoms are heart palpitations, feelings of
choking, chest pain, nausea, fear of losing control, dizziness, and difficulty breathing. Other symptoms include a sense of dread or impend-
ing disaster, and feelings of unsubstantiated terror and fear. Panic
attacks are unpredictable and unexpected, and signify an underlying
panic disorder. An initial panic attack comes out of nowhere and can
happen when an individual is doing some commonplace activity such
as eating in a restaurant, driving a car, or relaxing at home. Often
people with anxiety fear having another panic attack.

Depression

I am drowning in negativism, self-hate, doubt, madness . . .

—Sylvia Plath

Depression results from problems with chemical transmission in certain areas of the brain. The more severe forms of depression are believed to be genetic in nature. Depression also arises from experiencing
financial, emotional, or professional problems. Sometimes the person
blames himself for negative events from his past.

In Susanna Kaysen's *Girl, Interrupted,* Susanna speaks to her social
worker about what she wants to do:

> "A writer," I said when my social worker asked me what I
> planned to do when I got out of the hospital. "I'm going to be
> a writer." "That's a nice hobby, but how are you going to earn
> a living?"
> My social worker and I do not like each other. I didn't like
> her because she didn't understand that this was me, and I was
> going to be a writer.

The reaction of the social worker to Susanna's desire to be a writer makes her feel depressed, more than she already is. Depressed individuals need to be supported and encouraged, not put down or discouraged.

In the autobiographical novel *The Bell Jar,* Sylvia Plath writes about a young woman who becomes so depressed that she tries to kill herself and is institutionalized. The character is largely based on Plath's own personal bout of depression and her unsuccessful suicide attempt. In the novel Esther recovers, but the author eventually committed suicide.

Michael Cunningham's novel *The Hours* explores the lives of three different depressed female characters who come from different times in history, and how they relate, even though they're living in disparate circumstances and settings. The first character is Virginia Woolf, who is in the process of writing *Mrs. Dalloway* in 1925. The second character is Clarissa Vaughn, a middle-aged woman living in modern-day New York and planning a party for her friend Richard, who is dying of AIDS. He has nicknamed her Mrs. Dalloway. The third woman is 1950s housewife, Laura Brown—a pregnant, depressed young mother who is reading *Mrs. Dalloway.*

These characters are excellent examples of people suffering from depression and each responds to her sadness in a different way. In the following excerpt, you can see the depth of Virginia Woolf's despair as she contemplates suicide:

> She hurries from the house, wearing a coat too heavy for the weather. It is 1941. Another war has begun. She has left a note for Leonard, and another for Vanessa. She walks purposefully toward the river, certain of what she'll do, but even now she is almost distracted by the sight of the downs, the church, and a scattering of sheep, incandescent, tinged with a faint hint of sulfur, grazing under a darkening sky. She pauses, watching the sheep and the sky, then walks on. The voices murmur behind her; bombers drone in the sky, though she looks for the planes

and can't see them. . . . She herself has failed. She is not a writer at all, really; she is merely a gifted eccentric. . . . She has failed, and now the voices are back, muttering indistinctly just beyond the range of her vision, behind her, here, no, turn and they've gone somewhere else. The voices are back and the headache is approaching as surely as rain, the headache that will crush whatever is she and replace her with itself. . . . She reaches the embankment, climbs over and down again to the river. There's a fisherman upriver, far away, he won't notice her, will he?

Bipolar Disorder

And the heart that is soonest awake to the flowers is always the first to be touch'd by the thorns. *—Thomas Moore*

Bipolar Disorder, also known as manic depression, is an affective disorder that causes periodic mood swings in which the sufferer cycles from depression to mania. The bouts of depression may be characterized by difficulty in doing tasks, a short attention span, a decreased appetite, crying jags, difficulty in getting to sleep or sleeping too much, and in more severe cases, thoughts of self-harm. The manic stage is characterized by a decreased need for sleep, little self-control, overspending, increased sexual activity, irritability, rage, risk-taking, erratic and irrational outbursts. Bipolar disorder is a serious disorder of the brain and can be relieved through medications and psychotherapy. When you're creating a character suffering from bipolar disorder, be sure to show both moods and how he vacillates between them.

Antisocial Personality Disorders

Woe unto them that call evil good, and good evil; that put darkness for light, and light for darkness; that put bitter for sweet, and sweet for bitter! *—Isaiah 5:20*

Antisocial Personality Disorder is a disorder in individuals with a history of chronic antisocial behavior. The person has poor impulse control, shows cruelty to animals and people, is sexually promiscuous, physically aggressive, and has been in trouble with the law. Antisocial personalities don't conform with society's rules or laws. They are impulsive and irresponsible thrill seekers. They are indifferent to others' feelings, and lack complete empathy or compassion when hurting them. They ignore the rights of others and lack a conscience, and as a result, are considered to be exceedingly dangerous. Usually criminals display a type of Antisocial Personality Disorder, with the main characteristic being a complete disregard for the rights of others.

Psychopaths

As we saw in chapter six, psychopaths have antisocial personality disorder and are usually criminals, but not all people with antisocial disorder are psychopaths. Sociopaths have antisocial personality disorder, but they don't become serial killers and criminals. Yet, they do cheat, lie, steal, and manipulate.

Psychopaths have a lack of regard for the ethical rules or laws of society. They have a pervasive pattern of disregard for the rights of others and a failure to conform to social norms. They're irresponsible, nonconforming, apathetic to other people, and only concerned with their own needs, which they'll fulfill by any means, including pathological lying and manipulation. They don't develop meaningful relationships, are sexually promiscuous, and often abuse drugs and alcohol.

Some of them demonstrate these tendencies in childhood by being cruel to animals, torturing them, and even killing them. They usually have problematic or traumatic relationships with their mothers, who oftentimes are sexually promiscuous and even prostitutes. Serial killers exhibit the extreme in psychopathic behavior. Many serial killers have a childhood of maladaptive behaviors such as killing animals, torturing their siblings, lying, stealing, truancy, drugs, and alcoholism.

Let's look at an excerpt from Alice Sebold's *The Lovely Bones*. Here, readers get a glimpse of Mr. Harvey's childhood. At eight years old, Susie Salmon's future killer is already living a nomadic life of crime as his mother encourages him to help her shoplift:

> Getting caught became another moment in his life that brought fear—that sick feeling curling into his stomach like eggs being folded into a bowl—and he could tell by the closed faces and hard eyes when the person walking down the aisle toward them was a store employee who had seen a woman stealing.
>
> And she began handing him the stolen items to hide on his body, and he did it because she wanted him to. If they got outside and away in the truck, she would smile and bang the steering wheel with the flat of her hand and call him her little accomplice. The cab would fill with her wild, unpredictable love, and for a little while—until it wore off and they spied something glinting on the side of the road that they would have to investigate for what his mother called its "possibilities"—he did feel free. Free and warm.

Even at such an early age, Mr. Harvey's morals, values, and emotions are being shaped in an unhealthy, unnatural way. By using such vivid details and description, the author does an excellent job of establishing Mr. Harvey as a pathological and cunning liar and an unapologetic murderer. When you create psychopaths, be sure not to make them caricatures of mean monsters. Layer them with history and emotion, and you'll create truly frightening individuals.

Another good example of a fictional psychopath is the character Alex Forrest, played by Glenn Close, in the film *Fatal Attraction*. Married man Dan Gallagher, played by Michael Douglas, has a fling with Alex, a single unmarried woman, when his wife is away for the weekend.

While charming and delightful during their evening together, when he's ready to go home, Alex becomes unglued and attempts suicide. She also exhibits Borderline Personality Disorder traits. The transition of her character from a normal woman to a psychotic is shocking to Dan and the audience.

Throughout the film, Alex escalates her psychotic behavior to stalking, threatening, lying, and finally killing. As a psychopath, Alex's character is riveting, intense, narcissistic, repressed, and filled with rage. Lacking a conscience, her character keeps the audience in suspense and tension until the shocking ending. This is exactly what your character needs do if he's going to successfully engage readers.

Psychotics: The Uncommon Variety of Real People

"But I don't want to go among mad people," Alice remarked.
"Oh, you can't help that," said the Cat, "we're all mad here.
I'm mad. You're mad." *—Lewis Carroll*

Psychosis occurs when people suffer from extreme forms of mental illness. The psychiatric term for madness is psychosis, which is defined as a break or loss of contact with reality. The person often has delusions and hallucinations, and is impulsive and unresponsive to society and its rules or conventions. Psychotics suffer confused thinking and lose interest in their appearance. Some hear voices or see things that aren't there. Psychosis is an abnormal mental state, which is often progressive with a loss of mental functioning.

Schizophrenia

If you talk to God, you are praying; if God talks to you, you have schizophrenia. *—Thomas Szasz*

Schizophrenia is a form of psychosis characterized by dissociation, particularly between the intellectual processes. Schizophrenics often have psychotic breaks from reality and become disorganized and deteriorate. They suffer from delusions, hallucinations, disorganized speech, and incoherence. There are four subtypes for Schizophrenia:

1. **Paranoid Type:** Preoccupation with one or more delusions or auditory hallucinations.
2. **Catatonic Type:** Stupor or excessive motor activity that has no purpose; rigid posture or mutism.
3. **Disorganized Type:** Disorganized speech, disorganized behavior, and flat affect.
4. **Residual Type:** Absence of delusions, hallucinations, disorganized speech, and disorganized or catatonic behavior. Strange beliefs and experiences.

Paranoid schizophrenics are the type most commonly portrayed in books and films. The three other types are either completely catatonic—doing nothing—or so far removed from reality that they are not as effective to use with your characters.

The novel *I Know This Much Is True*, by Wally Lamb, portrays a character with paranoid schizophrenia, Thomas, and his unaffected twin brother, Dominick, the narrator of the novel. Thomas resides at the state mental hospital, and in this excerpt, his brother has signed him out to take him to breakfast:

Thomas and I had spent several hours together the day before. Our Sunday afternoon ritual dictated that I sign him out of the state hospital's Settle Building, treat him to lunch, visit our stepfather or take him for a drive, and then return him to the hospital before suppertime. At a back booth at Friendly's, I'd sat across from my brother, breathing in his secondary smoke and leafing for the umpteenth time through his scrapbook of clippings on the Persian Gulf crisis. He'd been collecting them since August as evidence that Armageddon was at hand—that the final battle between good and evil was about to be triggered. "America's been living on borrowed time all these years, Dominick," he told me. "Playing the world's whore, wallowing in our greed. Now we're going to pay the price."

He was oblivious of my drumming fingers on the tabletop. "Not to change the subject," I said, "but how's the coffee business?" Ever since eight milligrams of Haldol per day had quieted Thomas's voices, he had managed a small morning concession in the patients' lounge—coffee and cigarettes and newspapers dispensed from a metal cart more rickety than his emotional state. Like so many of the patients there, he indulged in caffeine and nicotine, but it was the newspapers that had become Thomas's most potent addiction.

Wally Lamb does a brilliant job of letting the readers learn the pain, delusions, and hallucinations of a paranoid schizophrenic, along with the frustration and love his twin brother feels for him.

Substance-Related Disorders

Courage is resistance to fear, mastery of fear—not absence of fear. —*Mark Twain*

Alcohol addiction or dependence can be measured by the following symptoms: needing increased amounts of alcohol to achieve an inebriated state; increasingly experiencing symptoms such as vomiting or hangovers; using larger amounts of alcohol and increasing the duration of drinking time; becoming a secret drinker and hiding your supply; being psychologically as well as physically addicted to alcohol; and suffering from physical ailments due to alcohol such as depression, sexual dysfunction, and mood swings.

In *The Lost Weekend,* a best-selling novel by Charles Jackson, the character Don Birnam is a writer having problems writing because of his alcoholism. The alcoholic character is realistically portrayed in all of his haze, his weekend bender, and his arrival in a detox ward of Bellevue Hospital, where he has hallucinations and escapes, just to spiral further down into a drunken stupor, despair, and depression. The author reveals the alcoholic's desperation to get a drink and the lengths he will go to just to soothe his demanding addiction. It is a character's journey into hell.

Drug addiction is defined as having a tolerance for a drug and needing ever increasing amounts of it to get an effect. When someone is addicted to drugs, she has withdrawal symptoms when trying to stop, takes the drug over longer periods of time than was prescribed, is preoccupied with acquiring the drug, and continues its use even when it begins to cause physical and psychological problems.

If you're creating characters who suffer from addictions, you need to understand that addictions are diagnosed as illnesses and be familiar with the different ways of treating them. Rehab, halfway houses, counseling, and twelve-step programs are all ways addicted characters can attempt recovery.

Warning signs of teen substance abuse are fatigue, red and glazed eyes, personality changes, mood swings, irritability, depression, lethargy, discipline problems at school, lowered grades, truancy, lack of interest in school work, change in music and dress, new friends, and problems with the law. Inhalant dependence, such as sniffing glue or aerosol spray cans, makes teenagers become intoxicated.

For an accurate portrayal of a teenage addict, check out *The Basketball Diaries,* written by poet Jim Carroll. His autobiographical account tells the story of his being a high school basketball star who descends into a world of drug addiction. He turns to robbing, shoplifting, and even mugging to get money to feed his ever-increasing drug habit. His addiction grows out of control, and his mother finally throws him out of the house. However, after almost dying, he turns himself around and gets into recovery.

If you want to create teenage characters who are involved with drugs, be sure to make them believable by showing the process of how they escalate from just experimentation with drugs to actually becoming an addict.

Pedophilia

Pedophilia is a sexual deviation in which an adult, male or female, seeks sexual gratification with a child or adolescent. These perpetrators are often insecure about their own sexuality and fear rejection from adult sex partners. They also have feelings of emotional immaturity and inadequacy.

A famous fictional pedophile is Humbert Humbert from Vladimir Nabokov's novel *Lolita*. Humbert is obsessed by "nymphets," and when he rents a room in the home of Charlott Haze, a widow, he is obsessed with her daughter, Lolita, a young school girl. Let's look at how Humbert Humbert seduces the twelve-year-old:

> My innocent little visitor slowly sank to a half-sitting position upon my knee. Her adorable profile, parted lips, warm hair were some three inches from my bared eyetooth; and I felt the heat of her limbs through her rough tomboy clothes. All at once I knew I could kiss her throat or the wick of her mouth with perfect impunity. I knew she would let me do so, and even close her eyes as Hollywood teaches.

Here, Nabokov not only shows Humbert's longing, but also reveals his sense of arrogance, as well as his perceptions of the child. When you create a pedophile character, keep in mind that most look like the next-door neighbor, an uncle, schoolteacher, or average person. In fact, many pedophiles are charming and seductive, and can manipulate children in seemingly innocent ways. They don't feel comfort-able with adult equals—only with children who they can control and have power over.

Gender Identity Disorders

Individuals with gender identity disorders feel as if they've been born with the wrong gender. The person feels more like the opposite sex. There are men who like to dress up in women's clothing and who identify with women more than men, and there are women who cut their hair and dress up like men. Many of these individuals become transsexuals, having a sex change operation and using hormones to enhance breasts or to become more muscular. The cause of the condition is unknown and the individuals often suffer from depression and an increased suicide rate.

A realistic characterization of gender identity disorder is in the film *Boys Don't Cry*. Based on a true story, the film depicts a young woman, Teena Brandon, who desperately wants to be a boy. She cuts her hair, puts a sock in her pants, and presents herself as a man named Brandon Teena after she moves.

Eating Disorders

Essential features of anorexia nervosa are that the individual doesn't maintain a minimally normal body weight, is intensely afraid of gaining weight, and exhibits a significant disturbance in the perception of the shape or size of her body.

Binge eating is eating an amount of food that is definitely larger than most individuals would eat in a period of time usually limited to less than two hours. A binge is not limited to a single sitting and typically includes sweet, high-caloric foods, and is characterized more by abnormality in the amount of food consumed than by a craving for a specific nutrient such as carbohydrates.

Bulimia nervosa is a pattern of binge eating and purging, in which the bulimic views himself as unable to control his eating, and feels guilty and angry after bingeing. Bulimics engage in self-induced vomiting after bingeing, although this is not a requirement for a person to be diagnosed with this disorder. They can also be diagnosed if they engage in any inappropriate weight control method such as misuse of laxatives, taking diuretics, persistent fasting, use of enemas, or excessive exercise.

Since characters with eating disorders are frequently portrayed in television movies, you'll need to be especially careful when creating your own character, or you could end up writing a clichéd character who isn't realistic or unique. Keep in mind that an eating disorder is a symptom of a deeper inner conflict and not the cause. There are various types of eating disorders and each one is manifested in a different way.

Cathi Hanauer's *My Sister's Bones*, does an excellent job of exploring the devastating effects of anorexia not only on the sufferer, but also on the entire family. *The Hunger*, by Point Jillian Medoff, also offers a wonderful look at a fictionalized account of the ravaging effects an eating disorder can have on an entire family. If you choose to create a character with an eating disorder, remember to keep in mind that these disorders are often symptomatic of deeper problems. As the author, it will be up to you root out these problems and develop them for readers.

Creating Emotionally Deep Characters

Direct your eye right inward, and you'll find / A thousand regions in your mind / Yet undiscovered.
—*Henry David Thoreau*

Hopefully, these troubled characters will help you begin to think of your own characters and what internal disturbances they're suffering.

Readers and viewers want to watch troubled characters from a distance. They become intrigued with and appalled by the desperation of troubled characters and hope each will eventually see the light at the end of the tunnel.

Don't write your autobiography, but write what you know or about people you know who've experienced the difficulties of life and come out on the other side. From addicts to abuse, from compulsions to delusions, these characters are colorful, courageous, and complex. Now that you have an overview of certain types of personality disorders and emotional problems, you're ready to create multifaceted and emotionally deep characters for your own novels, short stories, plays, or films.

lasting impressions: body language, dialogue, and subtext

The face is the mirror of the mind, and eyes without speaking confess the secrets of the heart. —*Saint Jerome*

*S*ince more than 93 percent of all communication is nonverbal, it is important to know how to develop the silent voices of your characters. In this chapter, you will get a better understanding of your characters' differences through their nonverbal communication. In order for you to create interesting and memorable characters, you need to give your characters a unique physicality, so in their silence they are sending information to others through their appearance, posture, body language, and nonverbal communication.

Nonverbal communication is anything you communicate without words. Listeners or receivers pick up cues unconsciously and make judgments about other people just from their appearance. When meeting people for the first time, you have approximately ten to twelve seconds to make an impression. Your first impression of another person is based on nonverbal communication. So, too, are the first impressions of your characters.

Nonverbal Communication

216

In the end, we will remember not the words of our enemies, but the silence of our friends. —*Martin Luther King Jr.*

There is no other human being in the world who is just like you. You

are one-of-a-kind, unique in all of your individual splendor. People
are different. They come in all shapes and sizes, heights and widths,
colors and characteristics. Not only are people different in their looks,
they are different in their types and temperaments. Your characters
also have unique temperaments and body types, which become part
of their nonverbal communication.

Temperaments

**Yond Cassius has a lean and hungry look; he thinks too much:
such men are dangerous.** *—William Shakespeare*

Since most individuals have an avid interest in other people, it's necessary for writers to know different aspects of an individual's personality.
People are born with different temperaments, and you'll want to become familiar with those different temperaments, so that you'll have
the ability to create original characters.

Greek scholar and father of medicine, Hippocrates, believed the
body has four humors. These four humors refer to four body fluids
responsible for determining each individual's moods. The four humors based on his personal observation are blood, black bile, ordinary
bile, and phlegm.

It's important for you to learn the characteristics of each humor
in order to create characters who contain different personalities, traits,
and temperaments. Individuals who have an ample blood supply have
a sanguine temperament. They are known to be cheerful and optimistic, and don't suffer from depression. An example of such a character
is Auntie Mame, the main character in *Round the World With Auntie
Mame*, a novel by Patrick Dennis. She is fearlessly optimistic even
when her circumstances are worrisome. Such persons are said to be
resistant to depression and are usually cheerful.

Those with too much black bile have black thoughts, are depressed,
and have a melancholic temperament. An example is the depressed

homeless man, Ratso Rizzo, in the film *Midnight Cowboy.* Many of Shakespeare's characters such as Othello, Richard III, and Macbeth have a melancholic temperament, which brings them to tragedy.

Individuals with too much ordinary bile have a choleric temperament. These people are usually too aggressive and impulsive. They often get into trouble because of their "hotheaded tempers." In Mario Puzo's *The Godfather,* the Don's son Sonny Corleone is so impulsive he doesn't use common sense, and his hair-trigger temper leads to his demise. Characters who are too aggressive are always getting themselves into trouble.

Characters with too much phlegm are usually cold people who are indifferent to things that excite others. Characters who have this type of temperament can be referred to as "cold-blooded" killers, or "cold-hearted," like Beth Jarrett, the mother in the novel *Ordinary People.*

Knowing the different temperaments will enable you to develop contrasting characters with varying moods and personalities. Most of your reader and viewers will be able to identify characters with these types of temperaments. Characters with diverse temperaments can create tremendous conflict in a story.

Consider your characters' temperaments before you write your story. You may want to create a muscular hero, a messy child, and a lean, starving artist. Or to be different, you could create an immaculate child, a fat hero, and a muscular artist. Each works if you realistically motivate their behavior. I always maintain that you can break the rules if at first you learn and understand them.

EXERCISE

Communication and Temperament

Create four characters with the different temperaments. Write either four separate scenes featuring each temperament or write one scene using four characters and all four tempera-

ments at the same time. How has giving a character a specific temperament helped your characters come to life? ■ ■ ■

Body Types

You can develop diverse and opposite characters by giving them distinctive body types. Dr. William H. Sheldon, a psychologist and physician, formulated a well-known personality theory based on a body-type approach. Sheldon's research showed the relationship between one's temperament and body type to one's personality. Sheldon referred to the three body types as endomorphy, mesomorphy, and ectomorphy.

A person whose physique is soft, flabby, and round is considered an endomorph. The endomorph could be a person who loves to relax, enjoys the good things in life, has a lot of friends, and eats well. He could be a bon vivant, like the fat, fun-loving Friar Tuck in *Robin Hood.*

Mesomorph body types are people who are well built and have a hard, muscular physique. Characters like Robin Hood, Superman, or Rambo are good examples of mesomorphs. Romantic heroes are usually mesomorphs because they're strong and muscular.

Ectomorph body types are individuals who are very thin and delicate in appearance. Blanche DuBois in *A Streetcar Named Desire* is fragile-looking and delicate, while Stanley Kowalski, her brother-in-law, is a muscular brute who falls into the mesomorph category.

EXERCISE
Communicating With Body Types

What body type are you? Answer the same question for your characters so that you're able to create characters who are not only contrasting in temperament but in looks as well. These different body types are excellent guides for you to follow when developing physiques for your characters. Create a scene with characters who have different body types. Do your characters behave differently from each other because of their body types? Were you able to give your characters conflict according to their body types and personalities? Go against the norm and create a hero who is an endomorph, a villain who is an ectomorph, or a heroine who is a mesomorph. How do these characters interact? How are the characters more original than if they followed a stereotypical body type? ■ ■ ■

Levels of the Self

A writer writes not because he is educated but because he is driven by the need to communicate. *—Leo Rosten*

There are four levels of an individual's self. Just as you operate from different levels in yourself, you must give your characters different levels from which to behave. By being familiar with these different levels of the self, you'll be better equipped to give your characters layers of contradictions and inner conflicts. The four levels are:

1. **The Public Self:** This is the level that you communicate to the world. When an individual speaks to you and acts in a certain way, you only see the tip of the iceberg. The public self is the part of the individual that is seen and heard. How do your characters represent their outer selves in dialogue and actions?

2. **The Private Self:** This is the emotional and internal world of an individual. How do your characters reveal their inner selves? Is it through acting depressed or being frightened? Do they hide what they're feeling on the inside and play a role? How congruent are your characters?

3. **The Fantasy Self:** This level is where daydreams, night dreams, and fantasies reside. What are some of the daydreams, night dreams, or fantasies that your characters have?

4. **The Ideal Self:** This fourth and final level of self wants perfection: "I want to be thinner, smarter, prettier, richer. I want to be more spiritual and more fulfilled." What are the ideals that your characters aspire to?

EXERCISE
Finding Your Character's True Self

Develop a character who looks caring on the outside, yet is unfeeling and detached on the inside. Understanding the different levels of the self can help you avoid stereotypical and clichéd characters, and build vibrant and dynamic ones. A character who looks mild and meek on the outside could be a hero in his fantasy or dream world in much the same way that **Walter Mitty** was in James Thurber's *The Secret Life of Walter Mitty.*

Next, refer back to the different levels of the self, and create a character who is completely different in her public persona than she is privately. Put her in a scene with another character who portrays himself in an incongruent way and let the sparks fly when these two characters reveal their true selves. ■ ■ ■

Body Language

Silence is as full of potential wisdom and wit as the unhewn marble of a great sculpture. —*Aldous Huxley*

Body language conveys more than what is being said. It includes facial expressions, stance, eye contact, grooming, body postures, hand gestures, personal hygiene, clothing, smell, tics, carriage, and hairstyles. These are all-important elements for you to consider when you're creating your characters because your characters are giving out wordless messages through these elements.

Body movements, such as shrugging shoulders, snapping fingers, pressing or pursing lips together, crossing arms tightly, tapping fingers, shaking hands, fidgeting, or tapping feet, reflect characters' emotions and feelings. Emotional nonverbal messages are more powerful than words. We spend endless time trying to decipher others' nonverbal communication to get clues about how they're feeling. Do they like me? Are they angry? Is she flirting with me? Are they unhappy? Are they bored?

If you're talking to someone and she looks at her watch, what is she communicating to you? If you're speaking to a friend and he looks at people over your head, what message do you get? If someone's tapping her foot, how do you think she's feeling? If a man is biting his pencil what does that tell you about his state of mind? What are the messages you infer from these nonverbal behaviors?

It's also important to note that the messages you infer or project have more to do with your state of mind and your sense of self. If you aren't feeling confident, you'll probably take complete responsibility for someone's behavior and most likely blame yourself. However, if you're having a great day and things are going well, if someone looks away as you speak, you probably won't think a thing about it.

When you create characters who interact with each other, you reveal who they are and how they feel about themselves through their actions and reactions. These wordless messages are important for you to study and learn, not only for yourself, but in order to create characters who come to life. You can't only write what characters think, say, or feel. You need to include what they do.

The secret of doing that is writing about the characters' nonverbal communication. For instance, if you write, "Susan was very angry," you are telling the reader how Susan is feeling. Instead, reveal how Susan expresses her anger through her nonverbal communication. "Susan glared at her boyfriend, standing with her arms akimbo. She grabbed a candy dish from the coffee table and flung it against the wall, breaking it into smithereens." Your readers know Susan's angry by her nonverbal language.

These examples should help you understand the importance of nonverbal behavior. When you create your characters, you'll now be aware of having them perform specific behaviors, rather than telling us how they're feeling. It's critical that you learn about and become aware of your own and others' nonverbal communication, so that you can show and not tell how your characters are feeling without words.

EXERCISE
Utilizing Nonverbal Communication Habits

223

What is your nonverbal communication—posture, dress, walk, gestures, eye contact, handshake? What do you say about yourself before you say anything? Now answer the same questions for your characters in your story. What is their nonverbal communication? How does she walk? What is her posture like? Does she slouch or have great carriage? When she speaks, does she have good eye contact? Does she look away when another character talks to her? ■ ■ ■

Dialogue (or What Your Characters Say)

The dialogue is short, sharp, and continuous. It is broken by the minimum of description and by no preaching.
—*William Graham Sumner*

Writers use dialogue to give information, move the story forward, and reveal character. If your dialogue doesn't fit into any of these categories, don't use it. Never write dialogue just for the sake of making small talk or having characters exchange pleasantries like, "How are you?" "I'm fine." Since you don't want to lose the reader's attention, all dialogue should have a purpose.

When you write dialogue, be certain to have the characters take turns in speaking, interrupt each other, and talk in shorter sentences. Don't give your characters long-winded speeches or monologues. You need to listen to the sound of each character's voice. Is the tone friendly or is it hostile? Is the voice loud or soft, whiny or firm, constantly asking for permission or confident? What about the grammar, dialect, and choice of words that he uses? What do your characters' verbal communication sound like? What is their tone of voice, volume, inflections, speech patterns, use of language, timbre, rhythm? It is important to give each of your characters a different voice so they won't sound alike. It's also important to portray the listening skills of a character through the existence of (or lack thereof) attentiveness, eye contact, stillness, and other reactions while listening.

A great way to make your characters sound different from one another is to use an adverb or adjective that best describes each character's major personality trait. Then use that same adverb or adjective when you're about to write their dialogue so that it is representative of their personality. If a character's most dominant description is arrogant, then make his dialogue sound arrogant. Use a character's attitude for his dialogue. If he is confident, then the dialogue should reflect that confidence. An insecure person might stutter, hesitate, and look for reactions from the listeners to get cues about how he's feeling. Maybe he hesitates or speaks softly, because he is frightened of saying the wrong thing. If you describe a character as aggressive, then make certain he sounds aggressive and his dialogue fits his personality. If you describe another character as shy and insecure, the way he talks should reflect his insecurity.

What do your characters sound like when they speak? Are their voices melodious? Do they talk too loud? Do your characters all sound different? Do some speak quickly and others draw out their words? Do some have a booming voice while others whisper? What are the rhythms of their words? Do your characters speak in a monotone? Do others whine when they speak?

EXERCISE

Developing Different Communication Styles

Be certain to give your characters different verbal styles so they won't all sound the same. Describe their verbal communication—tone of voice, speech patterns, use of language, inflections, timbre, tone, grammar, profanity, interruptions, pauses, and stuttering. Create a scene with several characters and have their verbal communication be distinctive and different

from one another. Remember to include their tone of voice, and let the dialogue fit the character. ▪ ▪ ▪

Subtext (or What Your Characters Don't Say)

Anger dwells only in the bosom of fools. —*Albert Einstein*

There are always other things going on inside a person while he is speaking. What are the feelings or actions beneath or in addition to the words? Subtext, or meta-message, refers to the underlying or hidden meaning of the message. What is the hidden message that isn't being said? For example, if you're on a date and a woman tells you she feels sorry for married couples and loves being single, is she warning you not to get too serious about her? What is hidden in that message? What's the subtext? If you don't take what she says at face value, maybe the subtext is the opposite, and she really feels sorry for herself because she's unmarried. Maybe she's playing hard to get by not acting interested in marriage, but in reality she desperately wants to be married.

I always tell my clients who are given messages like this that there's a meta-message being sent. Listen to what is not being said to get the real message. Listen to the silent voice of the other person.

The subtext of your characters' actions and feelings are much more important than their words. Subtext is the meaning behind the words or the emotions behind the actions. It is how most of us live our lives. If we did and said exactly how we felt, we'd probably end up with no friends or family. Give them subtext to use in place of direct dialogue. When you have your characters say one thing and mean another, it allows your audience to identify with them. You leave room for your audience to project their similar emotions onto the characters. If your characters are too direct or too on the nose in their speech, you don't allow your readers or viewers the space to bring in their own feelings and emotions, and your characters sound too melodramatic.

For example, in *Ordinary People* there is a scene in which the family is taking family pictures on Thanksgiving. The father, Cal, wants to take a picture of Conrad and his mother, Beth. But Beth says she wants to take the picture. Cal insists, while Beth resists. Finally, Conrad shouts, "Don't take the goddamn picture!" The subtext is that Beth really doesn't want to have her picture taken with Conrad, and he knows it. Not a word is spoken but everyone including Conrad knows the truth. Rather than having long speeches about the real facts, the camera incident reveals the subtext.

EXERCISE

Communicating Through Subtext

Think about the times throughout the day when you don't truly reveal your emotions through your dialogue or behavior. You will probably be amazed at how many times you feel one way and behave another. Or how many times you show your anger indirectly by giving dirty looks to the guy who cuts in front of you in traffic or by acting indifferent to somebody you really like. Make a notation in your journal every time you say and do something but really mean something else. You'll be surprised how much of your real self is hidden.

Now do the same thing for your characters. Notice how they say one thing and mean another. How many times do they act against what they're really feeling? Close your eyes and visualize what emotion you want to indirectly express through your characters' behavior or dialogue. Now write a scene in which two characters aren't being honest but acting one way while feeling another.

Next, write a scene between two or more of your characters, but instead of using a lot of words, try to communicate your characters' feelings through gestures, facial expressions, or body language. Use

these physical actions in place of dialogue and see how you bring your characters to life. ▣ ▣ ▣

Emotional Imagery

The rules of the imagination are themselves the very powers
of growth and production. The words, to which they are re-
ducible, present only the outlines and external appearances.
—*Samuel Taylor Coleridge*

Emotional imagery is the use of a group of words that appeal to the senses of touch, taste, sound, sight, and smell. Emotional imagery is imagery that evokes emotions. Reach deep inside yourself and allow your emotions to create emotional imagery for your characters. Try to use emotional imagery when creating your characters, so you can touch your readers and viewers in a deep way.

By using emotional imagery, you'll evoke feelings from your readers. You'll also want to make them feel empathy. Let your imagination and your deeper consciousness conjure up visual imagery that is emotionally meaningful to everyone. The more you listen to your inner voices, the more you open up your intuition and sensory memories, the more real your characters become.

Janet Fitch's *White Oleander* is named for a plant that is beautiful but poisonous. It creates an emotional image of Ingrid, the mother in the novel, who is beautiful but also dangerous and manipulative.

Visual images are powerful. The first motion pictures were silent, yet the characters were very real, and people rooted for the hero and rooted against the villain. The characters' goals came across to the audience without any words being spoken. What you see can touch you very deeply because feelings are attached to emotional imagery. Imagery such as darkness and light often stand for good and evil. Darkness and light can also be symbolic for life and death. Visual images create emotional reactions for your readers and viewers. A heroine can deliberately be dressed in white to give her an aura of innocence, while a villain can be clothed in black, which evokes an emotional response of fear or danger. Certain images of animals are emotionally charged and make people instantly react. The dove connotes peace or love; the raven, crow, and snake are images for evil or danger.

Joseph Conrad's *Heart of Darkness* is a story about a man, Marlow, who is searching in the jungle of Africa for a troubled man named Kurtz. The entire book is filled with emotional imagery and visual descriptions rich in texture and emotional tone. Here is a description:

> They were dying slowly—it was very clear. They were not enemies, they were not criminals, they were nothing earthly now—nothing but black shadows of disease and starvation, lying confusedly in the greenish gloom. Brought from all the recesses of the coast in all the legality of time contracts, lost in uncongenial surroundings, fed on unfamiliar food, they sickened, became inefficient, and were then allowed to crawl away and rest. These moribund shapes were free as air—and nearly as thin. I began to distinguish the gleam of eyes under the trees. Then, glancing down, I saw a face near my hand.

The images and descriptions are evocative to the reader and create painful and yet powerful emotional imagery. This is the type of imagery you want to write to create an emotional response from your readers.

EXERCISE
Using Imagery for Impact
Visualize your characters and describe them using imagery. Write a description of your characters by referring to them

through the way they're dressed and the images they create. Use all of your senses in your characters' description. However, don't overuse **emotional imagery because it'll lose its impact. Think in larger terms of what themes or concepts you want to impart through your images and be consistent.** ■ ■ ■

Interior Monologues

> The writer can only explore the inner space of his characters
> by perceptively navigating his own. —*Peter DeVries*

There is much more to creating characters than giving them a goal and having them overcome obstacles to reach it. As a creator of emotional characters, you want to build characters whose inner worlds can be revealed without them saying a word. Just like human beings, characters communicate more through their nonverbal communication than through their words.

Interior monologues can be used to have a character relate her thoughts inside her head. It adds intimacy and immediacy to your fiction. Interior monologue is used for the reader to better understand something about the character that the other characters aren't aware of. It is an organized train of thought that gives information to the reader.

Interior monologues are also used when a character has private thoughts that she doesn't reveal to the person she's speaking with. It's important for you to read examples of interior monologues, so you get a better understanding of how they are used—as an integral part of your dialogue that doesn't interrupt it but enhances it by giving further information.

Of course, when you're writing a short story or novel, you want to put your characters on stage and have the reader experience what the characters are experiencing at the very same time. You don't want to bog down your characters with interior monologues. However,

interior monologues are wonderful devices to use when you need your
audience to know what's happening behind your character's facade
and to learn the thoughts of the character at the same time she's
thinking them.

For example, in Jonathan Franzen's *The Corrections,* the author
writes about two elderly parents, Alfred and Enid Lambert, and their
three adult children. Enid wants to bring her children together for
one last Christmas. The father's interior monologue in this excerpt
paints a vivid picture of past memories:

> He was remembering the nights he sat upstairs with one or
> both of his boys or with his girl in the crook of his arm, their
> damp bath-smelling heads hard against his ribs as he read aloud
> to them from *Black Beauty* or *The Chronicles of Narnia.* How
> his voice alone, its palpable resonance, had made them drowsy.
> These were evenings, and there were hundreds of them, maybe
> thousands, when nothing traumatic enough to leave a scar had
> befallen the nuclear unit. Evenings of plain vanilla closeness in
> his black leather chair; sweet evenings of doubt between black
> nights of bleak uncertainty. They came to him now, these for-
> gotten counter examples, because in the end, when you were
> falling into water, there was no solid thing to reach for but your
> children.

The above excerpt is not only an example of interior monologue, but
also includes wonderful emotional imagery, especially the description
as follows: "Evenings of plain vanilla closeness in his black leather
chair; sweet evenings of doubt between black nights of bleak uncer-
tainty." These images evoke specific feelings of safety and fear at the
same time.

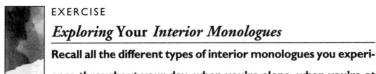

EXERCISE

Exploring Your *Interior Monologues*

231

Recall all the different types of interior monologues you experience throughout your day, when you're alone, when you're at work, when you're with friends, and when you are with your family. In your journal write how many times a day you criticize yourself. How many times in an hour do you worry about whether or not somebody likes or approves of you? Make a note of it. Who do you worry about? Is it your boss, your parents, your lover, your competitor? Note it in your journal. By doing this, you will get a greater awareness of how often you have interior monologues throughout your day, and, by extension, you'll be better equipped to provide your characters with realistic and revealing interior monologues of their own. ■ ■ ■

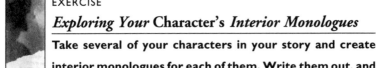

EXERCISE

Exploring Your Character's *Interior Monologues*

Take several of your characters in your story and create interior monologues for each of them. Write them out, and you'll be able to better understand each character's inner thoughts and internal feelings. Is your character critical of herself? Is your character preoccupied with herself and the impression that she's making? Keep creating interior monologues for all of your characters and get a better understanding of who they really are on the inside. ■ ■ ■

Gestures, Quirks, and Expressions

Outside show is a poor substitute for inner worth. —*Aesop*

A crucial element in all stories is not what the characters say, but what they express through body language, gestures, posture, dress, and eye contact. Nonverbal communication techniques between characters are the most powerful type of character development.

Moments of silence can speak volumes. Silence can be more powerful than long speeches. Some of the most memorable scenes between characters are those in which nobody talks. For example, in Henry Fielding's classic novel *Tom Jones*, there is a famous scene in which Tom and his beautiful female companion are eating a huge meal. They face each other as they eat and don't speak throughout. The scene takes on many layers of meaning, the least of which is food. Food becomes a metaphor for their sensual feelings toward each other.

You must not only think about who your character is, but also what she communicates about herself through her actions. What gestures or quirks do your characters have that are indigenous to them? Frowns, gestures, smiles, glares, ogling, dirty looks, leers, and sneers are all nonverbal expressions that convey many powerful meanings. It's just as important for you to plan your characters' nonverbal actions as it is your plot.

Dishonesty is often revealed by a person's body language through nervousness or tension. The way to detect when someone is lying is through certain cues people give without being aware of them. Lack of eye contact or looking away when speaking to someone engenders distrust. Body language such as fidgeting, shifty eyes, moving away, and blushing are gestures that give body cues that someone may be lying. Honest people are generally open and relaxed. Maintaining eye contact creates trust and gives them credibility.

A person with sociopathic tendencies doesn't feel guilt when he lies. However, someone who is not an experienced liar gives clues. The saying, "He wore a guilty expression on his face," shows that people can't always hide their guilt when they are lying or trying to hide something. Your characters' emotions leak out through their actions, whether they want them to or not.

Sometimes a character misinterprets the meaning of another character's actions and makes a false assumption through projection. For example, let's say a woman is at a party and sees a friend of hers. She waves to her friend, but he ignores her. The first thought she has is that he doesn't like her anymore. However, the reality could be that he can't see her because he's not wearing his glasses. So the meaning of this action is misinterpreted and could result in a rift in the characters' relationship.

The tone of voice and facial expressions can also unintentionally— or, perhaps intentionally—change the meaning of what is said, allowing for misinterpretations by listeners. If someone tells you how sorry he is for hurting your feelings and he has a smile on his face, the message you're receiving is confusing. What do you believe? The words or the facial expression? Often it's not what is being said, but how it's being said, which is the real message.

Nonverbal signs of stress can be as diverse as muscles tightening, nervous tics in the eyelid or face, unsteady hands, restlessness, clearing of the throat, sweating, skin rashes, and stiff posture. These mannerisms reveal a character's emotional state of being. You need to depict your characters emotions through facial expressions, their body, their stance, posture, and demeanor.

Decide in advance how you want to move your audience emotionally. What reaction do you want your audience to have? When you decide, you then have to anticipate and fulfill your audience's expectations. As we discussed earlier, finger tapping, hand shaking, stomach tightness, throat clearing, nail biting, foot tapping, hand wringing, swaying, nervous coughing, crossing and uncrossing legs, lip biting, sweating, and darting eyes are all great indications of a character who is feeling tense and nervous. Boredom can be expressed through yawning, not focusing, doodling, playing with objects, stretching, and looking away while another character is speaking. Nonverbal expressions of anger include throwing one's hands in the air, shaking one's fist, shaking one's head, making disgusted faces, rolling one's eyes, grimacing, shrugging, rapid breathing, scowling, and glaring.

EXERCISE

Letting the Action Do the Talking

Create an emotional state of being for several of your characters and put them in a scene. Without writing how they
feel, let their emotions come out through their actions. Create a
scene in which there is emotional conflict between some of the
characters. Were you able to indicate powerful emotions for your
characters by their actions? Keep observing people in your daily life
and incorporate new behaviors that reveal your characters emotional state of being. ▪ ▪ ▪

Looks Can Be Deceiving

> We can be redeemed only to the extent to which we see our-
> selves. —*Martin Buber*

When you're deciding on the characters you want to portray in your
story, keep in mind that external appearance will be a crucial point.
What is his age? Body type? Physical appearance? Is he handsome,
ugly, fat, or thin? Does he have characteristics such as tattoos, scars,
acne, and disabilities? Is he a rugged outdoorsman or a well-dressed
businessman? These are some of the external attributes you give to
your characters, so that they make a definite impression. Does your
character smile a lot, but feel furious on the inside? Smiling reveals
happiness, contentment, humor, warmth, friendliness, and approach-
ability. If your character frowns or grimaces he could be expressing
anger, negativity, impatience, or frustration.

What do your characters say about themselves externally? What
are your characters saying about themselves without saying anything?
Are they confident, arrogant, insecure, worried, angry, happy, tenta-
tive, shy, aggressive, assertive, positive, or negative? You can deliberately build an image to make a definite impression. You can do the
same thing for your characters—create an image for them to suit your

plot. How many times have you read about or seen a mousy-looking female character with horn-rimmed glasses who wears her hair in a top knot, suddenly loosen her hair, take off her glasses, and turn into a beauty queen?

Your characters' physical appearance will create a difference in the roles they play in your story. What are they saying through their physical appearance? First, you can easily decide what part you want your character to play by the way he or she looks. If you want to create a female character who is petite and weighs ninety pounds or a woman who is six feet tall and weighs two hundred pounds, you are definitely creating two distinct characters, even if you give them the same goals.

A character who is handsome and virile-looking will probably be the hero or love interest in your story, while a quiet scientist who is thin and wears glasses will usually not be a love interest in your story. (Of course, it might be a more interesting story if he is the love interest.) You also need to decide about your character's personal hygiene. Does he have body odor, bad breath, an unkempt appearance, or greasy hair? Your filthy character certainly will be treated differently from a character who practices cleanliness and good grooming.

Concentrate on how a character walks and on her mannerisms, behaviors, gestures, and posture. You can tell a lot about a character's frame of mind by the external way she presents herself. How does she package herself through her dress, demeanor, and hairstyle? Does she emit positive or negative energy? Does she look happy or sad?

It's important for you to understand how the physical attributes you give your characters are just as critical as their inner drives. Whatever goals you set up for your characters, it's their physical appearance that will determine how they'll behave in the plot. A child who is handicapped acts differently from an athletic child, even if they have the same goal. Each of the above characters would have a different story to tell, although they are on the same journey.

Appearances Speak Volumes

We know what a person thinks not when he tells us what he thinks, but by his actions. —*Isaac Bashevis Singer*

You want your audience to care about your characters and be curious about how they're doing. Your characters must be believable—that is essential. Readers need to be involved with and connected to them. The way a character walks gives a lot of information about him. Brisk walking expresses determination; slouching or slumping with poor posture can express lack of confidence or sadness; walking cautiously, darting eyes, and a tense facial expression can indicate fear. Listen to the music of your characters—their facial expressions, mannerisms, tone of voice, volume, eye contact or lack of it. Nonverbal communication speaks volumes more than dialogue.

How good are you at reading other people? Do you know what they're feeling by the expression on their face? Does the way a person holds tension in his body let you know when he's upset? Can you read cues from others' nonverbal communication? Are you able to identify the emotions they are revealing through their nonverbal actions? How good are you at imagining what they're feeling? Are you able to create a story for them by the way they communicate without speaking? Ask yourself if your character is deferential, if he wants to please, or if he's indifferent.

You want your readers and viewers to be fascinated by your characters. You'll achieve this by giving your characters distinction, individuality, and originality. Appearances are deceiving, and you can create an interesting character by giving her an offbeat appearance or one that's against type.

Part of what makes up your characters' overall appearance is their dress. Fifty percent of what you see when you first meet someone is what they're wearing. There's a saying that "Clothes make the man." Well, although it's not entirely true, you can be impressed with or turned off by the way your characters dress. Some dress conservatively; others are sloppy. Some characters look chic and wear the latest fashion, while others wear used clothing from the thrift shop. What impression do you want your characters to make through the way they dress? Think about how you dress differently for different occasions.

In the following excerpt from Bret Easton Ellis's *American Psycho,* the narrator, Patrick Bateman, describes his date as she enters the room. From the description you can get a visual image of this character's wealth, her class, and what she says about herself without speaking:

> She arrives thirty minutes late and I tell the doorman to let her up even though I meet her outside my door while I'm locking it. She isn't wearing the Karl Lagerfeld suit I expected, but she looks pretty decent anyway; a silk gazar blouse with rhinestone cuff links by Louis Dell'Olio and a pair of embroidered velvet pants from Saks, crystal earrings by Wendy Gell for Anne Klein and gold sling-back pumps.

If you go on a job interview with a large corporation, you probably wouldn't choose to wear a miniskirt and platform heels. Instead, you'd dress for the part. If you were interviewing with a production company in Hollywood, you could probably be much more casual than if you were interviewing with a corporate law firm. If you're dressing to impress, you might wear a power suit and carry a briefcase. You need to be aware of the impression you want your characters to make in your story and dress them accordingly. Put them in situations and let them dress according to the image you want them to create.

 EXERCISE
Impressions, Appearances, and Nonverbal Communication

It's important to first consider what type of impression you want your character to make and to then choose clothes that make

that impression. **Decide on what image you want to give your main character and the antagonist of your story. Create the clothing that you want each one to wear, so that both can be identified by their appearance. Describe them in detail from their hair down to their shoes. After you've completed dressing your characters, do they each reflect the appearance you want them to have? If not, keep working until you get it right.**

The importance of nonverbal communication for bringing your characters to life is invaluable. Now that you have all the necessary nonverbal techniques to let your characters come alive through their silent voices, you'll be successful every time you create characters for any type of book, film, or play you write. Remember, it's not what your characters say, it's what they don't say that is the real powerful message. Just listen to their silent voices and breathe life into your characters! ■ ■ ■

Index